D1311900

Everyday Dress

1650–1900

Happy crowds enjoying the seaside in Ramsgate Sands, 1852, but dressed as for town; no beachwear then. By W. P. Frith, notable as a recorder of the Victorian scene.

Everyday Dress
1650–1900

Elizabeth Ewing

Chelsea House Publishers
New York
Philadelphia

**Published in the USA by
Chelsea House Publishers.
Printed and Bound in Mexico**

7   9   8

ISBN 1-55546-750-4

Contents

Acknowledgements

Picture Acknowledgements

Grateful acknowledgement for permission to reproduce illustrations is made as follows:

Reproduced by gracious permission of Her Majesty the Queen: frontispiece
Cheltenham Museum: 93; Fashion Research Centre, Bath: 8, 25, 29, 30, 52, 53, 55, 56, 95; Mansell Collection: 1, 2, 3, 4, 7, 9, 10, 11, 12, 13, 15, 16, 18, 19, 20, 21, 26, 27, 28, 31, 32, 33, 34, 35, 38, 42, 43, 51, 54, 58, 62, 64, 71, 72, 73, 74, 75, 76, 77, 78, 81, 84, 86, 87, 89, 96, 99, 100, 102, 103, 104, 105, 109, 111, 112, 118, 119; Publisher's Collection: 22, 23, 24, 36, 37, 44, 49, 65, 66, 69, 70, 88, 91, 106, 108, 110, 114, 115, 117; Renfrew District Museums and Art Galleries: 63; Science Museum: 5, 40, 41; Staffordshire County Museum Service: 46, 48, 113, 116; Victoria & Albert Museum: 6, 17, 45, 47, 50, 57, 59, 60, 61, 67, 68, 94, 97, 98, 107; Doreen Yarwood (from *The British Kitchen*, published by B. T. Batsford): 79, 83; University of Reading, Institute of Agricultural History and Museum of English Rural Life: 80

General Acknowledgements

Because of its subject this book has called for material from a number of sources outside the normal ambit of costume history. For guidance, help and information I have been deeply and constantly grateful to Doreen Yarwood, whose widespread, immensely varied but closely co-ordinated studies of many aspects of human activity have been invaluable to me in dealing with the many factors apart from fashion which have always influenced the dress of ordinary people.

I am also greatly indebted to the librarians and staffs of the London College of Fashion and Clothing Technology and of the Uxbridge and Ruislip (Manor Farm) libraries for their generous help in locating and giving me the use of many books not easily accessible.

Penelope Byrde, Keeper of Costume at the Museum of Costume, Bath, has provided invaluable help in suggesting many illustrations from the excellent resources of the Costume Research Centre there and in giving me permission to use a number of illustrations not otherwise available. The staff of the Mansell Collection most patiently and enterprisingly located material for illustrations in scores of files. Many local museums also responded very cordially to requests to reproduce items in their possession.

I
The Early Ways

Dress Versus Fashion

Costume historians and students of dress have always tended to devote most of their attention to fashionable clothes. To do so is natural. Fashionable dress aims at attracting attention. It has always been the style of dress favoured at a certain time and place by a privileged group or class proclaiming its special identity by its choice of clothes. Such clothes were valued and treasured and often kept for posterity. It follows that such fashionable clothes of the past constitute almost exclusively the costume collections displayed in museums and art galleries and preserved by costume collectors. They provide most of the material of most costume histories, written and illustrated. Most of the best known portraits of individuals in past centuries show royal, notable or fashionable people attired in their best clothes.

Clothes, however, have a far wider context than this. Clothes before anything else differentiate mankind from the animal world. They have always been to some degree the concern of every human being. They affect human dignity and self-respect whatever the rank or status of the wearer and therefore they influence and reflect his place in society. But relatively few people through the centuries in any country have worn fashionable dress, or have been able to do so. The majority of ordinary people have to work to live, to provide themselves with shelter and food and clothes and the other appurtenances of life out of money that is usually limited. They wear ordinary clothes and such clothes have a story of their own which is too little told; indeed it is very difficult to tell. The clothes were normally worn out. The idea of keeping them did not normally occur to people.

Social history, dealing with ordinary people, has only in the last century engaged substantial attention and dress has not generally been a main part of it.

The subject of ordinary clothes is vast. Potentially, it covers occupational clothes – those worn for specific kinds of work, uniforms of all kinds, and it could range from almost the top to the bottom of society. But for most people today and yesterday ordinary dress means the kind of clothes worn by the man or woman 'in the street', by the general mass of people going about their business or other daily activities, working for their living, or at leisure or play. What did they look like? What were their clothes made of? How and where did they get them? One thing that is certain is that ordinary clothes bore little resemblance to what was decreed by fashion, not least because the range of clothes available to the ordinary wearer at one time and place was extremely restricted.

If the art of past centuries, and collections of dress, are generally reflections of high fashion, how can we know what ordinary people wore? Fortunately, so far as England was concerned, from the later seventeenth century onwards a rich store of personal diaries, memoirs, letters and personal histories survives and records in considerable detail the ordinary life of the times, including much about dress. Many writers go into the subject in considerable detail and write with an ease and intimacy which come undulled across the centuries – perhaps the more so because often they wrote with no thought of posterity or even of publication; only by accident have many such writings been preserved.

The period covered by this book, the two-

and-a-half centuries from 1650 onwards, has a unity of evolution, covering in most respects the rise and development of what we commonly call the modern world – a world of national growth and expansion, exploration and discovery, science and invention, economic and industrial progress on a scale never before seen: a world of new ways of life for its inhabitants, of new social structures and class distinctions. Something of what such changes meant is reflected in everyday terms by changes in the dress of ordinary people which reveal, consciously or unconsciously, much about the circumstances in which they lived and their attitude to them. Local archives sometimes contribute further information. As the whole period is one of an increasing rise in the numbers and importance of the middle and lower classes and of increasing attention being given to ordinary people and their affairs, the picture becomes increasingly clear as it progresses. It was such people, making their way in the world by their own efforts, geared up to the increasingly varied activities of the professions, business, trade, science, invention, who were to set the main pattern of everyday dress.

Materials for Ordinary Clothes

From earliest times four natural fibres, cotton, flax, silk and wool, used in a great variety of forms, have been the mainstay of the dress of mankind everywhere. Not till the present century's vast contrivance of man-made fibres has the ages-old pattern been disturbed and in many ways the ages-old natural materials are as strongly enthroned as they have ever been.

1 *Early spinning and weaving, from a twelfth-century manuscript in Trinity College, Cambridge.*

8

The spinning of yarn and the weaving of cloth were the first crafts of all to be practised by early man and century by century, in country after country, they retained many of their original features. Even today some processes have close affinities with the remote past and are living history. This continuity was very strong in the seventeenth century, when developments had been great but traditional processes had not been transformed at any point by mechanization.

How, when and where the processes of spinning and weaving were first devised are all unknown. The earliest known evidence lies in the Bronze Age, reached at different times in different parts of the world. Archaeologists have gone as far back as 4500 BC in dating some pieces of linen found in Egypt, the earliest civilization to be recorded with any certainty. Linen, cotton and wool were all available there and used there for spinning and weaving, wool being the material most widely used for clothing by ordinary people, as in many other countries throughout history. In Britain in particular wool was not only important in ordinary dress but wool and wool textiles were Britain's first and main product for export and therefore a vitally important source of growth and development and rising national wealth.

The earliest known example of weaving in Britain consists of some pieces of a rough wool material ascribed to about 2000 BC and excavated in 1878 from a funeral barrow at Rylestone in Yorkshire, where they had been preserved miraculously by being kept dry in an oak coffin.

How weaving started in Britain is unknown; the perishable nature of the cloth and of the wooden appliances first used for spinning and weaving have defeated investigation. The lake villages of Meare and Godney, near Glastonbury in Somerset, have yielded the earliest surviving evidence. Built on stilts on a large lake known as Meare Pool, they flourished from about 250 BC to AD 50. Though drained about 1717, the site was not excavated until the 1890s, when these remarkable villages were dis-

covered, preserved by local peat and containing evidence of a community of fishermen, farmers and hunters. Among the relics found and now in Glastonbury Museum are spindle whorls, weaving combs, loom weights and bobbins of this period showing considerable expertise.

It is known that these people kept flocks and herds of animals; and sheep were indigenous to Britain, running wild in the forests which covered most of the country. The type was a small, black-faced one similar to some still found in St Kilda, the Shetland Islands and outlying districts of Wales, Scotland and Ireland.

From the beginning wool was established as the main material for spinning and weaving. Cotton did not grow in Britain, so was not used till it could be imported. Flax grew in a few areas, but was much more difficult to spin and weave than was wool, and also was much less useful for an agricultural populace living in a cool or cold climate. Silk was an ancient monopoly of the East, a scarce luxury probably first brought to England by returning Crusaders in the Middle Ages.

2 *Wheel for spinning and bobbin-winding, about 1300, drawn from the Luttrell Psalter in Trinity College, Cambridge.*

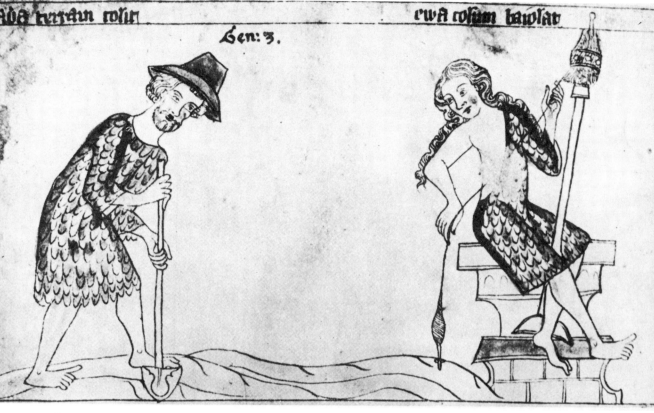

Gen: 3.

3 *'When Adam delved and Eve span'; from the Verislav Bible, 1340.*

There is some evidence that a wool trade with the Phoenicians existed in Britain before the Romans came. The latter brought new skills to the craft and exported cloth to Italy, where wool was the material most in demand for dress by all classes. After them the Anglo-Saxons played their part in fostering the development of trade in wool with Europe, which flourished between the eighth and the eleventh centuries. The Normans pursued the same policy and looked to a growing home and overseas trade in wool and woollen fabrics as the main basis of the economic expansion on which they were intent. Subsequent rulers had the same policies, Edward I and III being particularly active in this direction.

Britain's economic progress was therefore in many respects increasingly linked with the wool trade. What amounted to legal enforcement to wear wool was provided by the enactment from the fourteenth to the early seventeenth centuries of a series of sumptuary laws placing many restrictions on the type of dress permitted to the general populace. Sumptuary laws, governing personal habits and behaviour, as distinct from the general regulation of society by law, are strange to modern thinking but were an accepted part of the hierarchical society which prevailed all through the Middle Ages and after them, upholding the belief that class distinctions should be preserved in the interests of the stability of the state and that social climbing should be discouraged. Such laws specified that only people above a certain rank or possessed of a specified income should be allowed to wear rich fabrics, fine furs, embroidery, jewels and many other costly adornments, most of them imported. The privileged were few in number and while it appears that sumptuary laws were often flouted, they acted as a further stimulus to the wool trade.

Linen was used to a small extent by ordinary people, mostly the more privileged who could afford to employ it for trimmings and accessories and for the shifts and shirts which were the only generally worn items of underwear. By the seventeenth and eighteenth centuries linen was coming into more general use for these purposes, and also for collars and cuffs, women's tippets and caps and men's 'bands' or neckwear. Cotton, which had to be imported, was scarce and did not play any substantial part in everyday dress until imports soared in the latter part of the eighteenth century.

The immense growth of the wool trade took place in an England as yet untouched by industry, dominated by agriculture; a seventeenth-century England in which sheep were still England's richest agricultural product. In the process of growth and expansion England had moved far from being a simple rural community where 'Adam delved and Eve span'. But the spinning and weaving continued with ever-increasing impetus. Most of the spinning was still a cottage industry, carried on mainly by the women and children of the household; but now they worked not only for their own clothing and other needs but also for an ever-growing market at home and overseas.

The weaving had for the most part gone out of the four walls of every home. It took six spinners to keep one weaver fully employed, so when spun the yarn was increasingly bought by an entrepreneur, a dealer who concentrated on supplying spun yarn to full-time weavers. By this means growing home and overseas markets could be supplied.

In the course of this development cloth production had also moved far from the original weaving of rough homespuns and now embraced a great variety of fabrics, most of them indigenous to certain areas and even particular towns. East Anglia specialized in baizes (plain

4 *Spinning and weaving, c.1520; a family affair carried out in the home.*

woollen fabrics) and worsteds, the south-west was noted for its high-quality broadcloths which were being sought by the wealthier classes and which also 'clothed the fine gentlemen and rich merchants of half Europe' by the seventeenth century. The north was homelier, with an output of rougher types of woollens worn by ordinary people in the country and in the growing towns. Chief of them were kersey (a coarse wool) and fustian (a mixture of wool and linen or cotton). From records dating from the sixteenth century there emerges a kind of local history of fabrics. Thus drugget (closely woven wool) and cantel were products of Bristol; serges of Taunton and Exeter; linsey-wolsey (linen and wool) of Kendal; shaloon (twilled worsted), for linings, of Newbury. Welsh flannel, according to tradition originally used by William the Conqueror, continued to flourish throughout the centuries.

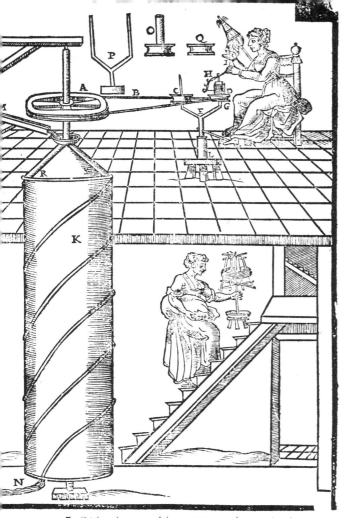

5 *Spinning machine, 1529, using water power.*

The increasing wealth of Britain in the latter part of the seventeenth century had a considerable effect on the structure of society. It meant that the ordinary man, even if he started in poor circumstances, could now look forward to a prosperity and status hitherto improbable. As early as the beginning of the century this had begun to be apparent. John Stow in his *Survey of London* (1603) had noted, 'in wealth, merchants and some of the chief retailers have first place' and Philip Stubbes made a similar comment. The tradesman became a worthy and dignified member of the community, mixing with the gentry and even enjoying the possibility of marrying into titled families.

The Role of the Tailor

The shaping of garments to the body, by cutting the cloth and stitching the pieces together and the creation of clothes of innumerable shapes either to fit the body or to change its shape for various reasons, practical or decorative, is almost entirely a western innovation of not many centuries' duration; it is implicit in the western concept of dress in general and not only of fashion.

This view of dress introduces a new figure, the tailor. He is so basic to western dress that Leslie Hunter and Margaret Stewart, the authors of *The Needle is Threaded*, the authoritative history of the clothing industry, declare sweepingly at the outset, 'A full history of the tailor would embrace the whole story of civilization. There is no older craft.'

Before the seventeenth century tailors operated at all levels, from the exclusive and

6 *The early tailor in his shop, cutting a garment; his workers are busy in the background. Frankfurt, 1568.*

fashionable, with premises in the elegant shopping centres of London and later of the main provincial towns, to village and itinerant craftsmen, the latter travelling the country with their equipment and visiting their customers, like the daily dressmakers of more recent times.

The claim that his was the first craft is also put forward for the tailor by R. Campbell in *The Complete London Tradesman*, 1747. It details 300 trades and admits only one possible forerunner of the tailor in the shape of Prometheus, arguing that as the tailor had to have a needle before he could ply his craft, fire and metal must have come first. (In fact the first needles were probably made of animal bone, so this point is not admissible.)

In practical terms Campbell recalls that the tailors of England formed one of the earliest trade guilds, were originally known as 'cissotii', and collectively were described as the Fraternitatis Cissorum. They had acquired a high degree of skill by the seventeenth century and consisted of master tailors, journeymen and apprentices. Journeymen were sometimes employed by the more prosperous master tailors and sometimes worked on their own, in town or village or travelling from place to place. Apprentices went through an organized training. The tailors can have had no easy task, because paper patterns for clothes as we know them did not exist until the seventeenth century. The earliest recorded tailors' patterns are in Spanish books and are dated 1589 and 1618. The French *Le tailleur sincère* is dated 1671.

The tailor was an important member of society by the seventeenth century, working for both men and women, skilled enough to make his own patterns for the very elaborate clothes often seen in paintings. He by no means worked only for the wealthy and privileged and he played a large part in the dress of all who could afford to keep up any kind of creditable appearance. From account books and general allusions it appears that ordinary people employed him, and that he was not usually highly paid. The amounts he received are regularly far less than those given for cloth, linings, buttons and trimmings, which were all normally provided by the customer.

Where to Shop in Restoration Times

Where did people acquire not only the cloth to be made up by the tailor but also the trimmings, accessories, gloves, stockings, hats and so forth? Country people – and the great majority of people came into this category in the seventeenth century – depended mainly on the great variety of pedlars and travelling salesmen who went the rounds of an area, calling at houses great and small, and on purchases made at fairs and markets, held from time immemorial at certain places, usually at fixed times, weekly, monthly or seasonally. All these were as old as history, and to tell the history of pedlars and fairs would need volumes to do it justice. The first shops probably came into existence when pedlars and other salesmen found enough customers in one place in a growing society to justify setting up a permanent location where customers would come to them.

In Britain, London had a long lead in this respect. By the seventeenth century shopping was well established and had achieved considerable variety. London Bridge, the only one crossing the Thames until Westminster Bridge was built in 1750, had two close-packed rows of shops all along its length before the Great Fire and these were bigger and better in the speedily rebuilt capital. All round the area, the hub of the smaller London of Restoration times, with a population of half a million, streets and areas were given over to certain specific ranges of goods, often given abiding names such as Threadneedle Street and Petticoat Lane.

Dress played a prominent part in this early shopping precinct. Mercers, ladies' tailors (who were men, of course) and lacemen clustered in Paternoster Row, drapers and booksellers were cheek-by-jowl in St Paul's churchyard and its environs. Cheapside was full of shops selling tempting accessories. On London Bridge fashion goods predominated. In the new London there was a start of the westward trend which has been a feature of London shopping ever

7 *An old London shop, before 1700.*

since, with the New Exchange in the Strand becoming a particular centre of attraction for the small purchases increasingly sought after in the new mood of easy, informal enjoyment of the passing moment which was a feature of Restoration England. This enjoyment extended to a much greater variety of people than in the past. From the times after the Fire, Covent Garden and Holborn began to be drawn into the shopping network.

The shops, however, remained small, sometimes consisting of the ground floor of the owner's home, with a window enlarged to provide a display of his wares. This continued through most of the eighteenth century. In addition to the multifarious shops there still remained even in London a motley array of pedlars, hawkers and street traders of all kinds, most of them dealing in small items, like pins and ribbons, but including second-hand clothes, which amounted to a vast section of the clothing trade, as will be shown later.

London, in the middle of the seventeenth century, was the Mecca of shopping for the whole of England, supplying the needs of people not only of the upper but also of the growing middle classes. Visiting friends from the town would be given commissions by rural people. Requirements, from tailor-made clothes for men to caps and bonnets for women, would be ordered by letter. As transport to and from London improved this traffic increased. Only gradually did other towns acquire shops that could to any extent compete with the capital. In the seventeenth century almost the only ones to do this were the two next largest towns, Bristol and Norwich, with populations of about 30,000 each.

8 *Traditional working people's everyday dress, seventeenth century; above, left to right, the tailor, the mower; below, the butcher.*

2
Living in the Late Seventeenth Century

The Account Book of Sarah Fell

Something of how people living the ordinary lives of the late seventeenth century, with limited money and time to devote to clothes, dealt with dress problems for themselves and their families, is shown in unexpected ways by recollections and records which some of them left. These are varied and considerable.

For a backward view from an isolated part of the north country towards the end of the seventeenth century a useful item is Sarah Fell's account book, unique as an outline documentary of the kind of life she led. To give it its full title, *The Household Account Book of Sarah Fell of Swarthmoor Hall* was never meant for publication and survived by a happy series of chances; it was not published in full until 1920, though it deals with five years of the 1670s.

It is a large book of 600 pages, 510 of which

9 *The pedlar remained unchanged for centuries and was a familiar sight all over Britain.*

form the actual accounts kept for each member of the family (three sisters and often the mother). It records in detail every imaginable kind of payment made for house, family, servants and farming activities. A wealth of information emerges on what the Fells wore; the account book details every item. The first entry was made on 25 September 1673, the final one on 15 August 1678. Those relating to purchasing clothes appear cheek by jowl with everything else, from eggs to horseshoes, candles to carpentry, sheep shearing to chimney sweeping, pigs to postage.

The Fells do not attempt to be self-supporting in the old way. They seem to have grown hemp and kept their own sheep for wool, but they regularly pay for spinners and weavers. There is an entry for 'milling and dressing 12 yds wt. kearsey of oures'. They also pay for the knitting of 'stockens' and for 'washing and rinshinge', which presumably means their household laundry. They make innumerable purchases of many kinds of cloth – 'kearsey', fustian, 'callicue' (calico), Cumberland cloth, 'sasnett' (a soft silk), holland, and also buy 'ribbins', tapes, thread, buttons. Their regular tailor, 'Math ffell' (Matthew Fell), appears 59 times in the accounts. He was a local man, living near Ulverston, and he worked for all the women of the family, as was usual during the seventeenth century where tailored items were concerned, even among those of limited means. Women dressmakers scarcely existed. The amounts paid to him vary from a few pence to several shillings, usually entailing work for several people. What was done was usually described merely as 'worke', though occasionally a 'wastcoate' or coat is specified.

The Fells also buy hats, gloves, shoes and clogs. They pay for footing their 'stockens'. They buy hemp for shirts and shifts, but after spinning and weaving these presumably were made at home, as was usual until the nineteenth century. Sarah from time to time sends petticoats to Kendal to be dyed, and other 'dieing' also goes there. Although she became a Quaker, Sarah did not feel bound to wear only austere, dark colours. She bought green ribbons, and had stockings dyed sea-green and sky-blue.

From the fact that so many purchases are made from surrounding towns and villages it appears that shopping facilities were not available locally. The biggest suppliers are in Lancaster, 20 miles away across two tidal estuaries. Gloves sometimes come from London. Cloth for the tailor often comes from Kendal. Many items of clothing were made for servants, as was customary at the time and for a considerable time to come. Stores also came from Kendal.

The account book demonstrates that 'a large proportion of the food and clothing for the ordinary family was provided entirely by the women and children'. Women played an important part in the household, being responsible for the dairy, orchard, garden, the management of pigs and poultry, the spinning of wool and flax and the brewing of beer.

A Traveller's View of Textiles

Starting little more than a decade after Sarah Fell's record and continuing into the next century (although not published until 1947) was *The Travels of Celia Fiennes*. It was forward-looking, outward-looking, a paeon of praise for England's progress, seeking to 'add much to its Glory and Esteem in our eyes', to improve trade and the general good.

Celia was an astonishing woman who from the late 1660s travelled on horseback through most of England with an acutely perceptive eye for every kind of fact and detail: in 1702 she wrote it all down. The result was the first comprehensive survey of England since Harrison's and Camden's in Elizabethan times and for the present purpose it is treasure trove, dealing as it does with spinning and weaving, the buying and selling of cloths, markets, fairs and the intensely lively, ever-growing wool trade of pre-industrial England at a time of great social and political changes.

The first version was called *Through England on a Side Saddle in the Time of William and Mary* and that is what it is. Celia's name is on the title page. She had companions, but men-

10 *Haymaking in the early seventeenth century;
an illustration for a ballad.*

tions only two servants, and also spare horses,
but she does not say how many. She gives no
details of herself, but her main travels were
during her thirties. Of her clothing she mentions
only a dust-coat and 'night cloths and little
things'. But she gives a profusion of first-hand
information of what she saw. with sharp observation of mining, drainage, agriculture as well
as cloth manufacturing, particularly of wool
processing, from weaving to marketing, all over
England.

She notes that, 'The ordinary people both in
Norfolk and Suffolk knit much and spin, some
with the rock and fasoe as the French does
[distaff and spindle], others at their wheeles out
in the streets and lanes as one passes.' She
describes the fulling or finishing of wool cloth
and flax-growing near Moreton-in-the-Marsh in
Gloucestershire. In East Anglia she goes to
Wymondham, 'where you meet the ordinary

people knitting four or five in a company under
the hedges'. At Derby 'they make great quan-
tetys of gloves. I did not observe or learn any
other trade or manufacture.'

She goes on to Leeds, 'a large town . . . this is
esteemed the wealthyest town of its bigness in
the Country, its manufacture is the woollen
cloth the Yorkshire Cloth in which they are all
employ'd and are esteemed very rich and very
proud'.

Colchester 'is a large town', which specializes
in making the plain woollen fabric called Bayes;
'great quantities are made here and sent in
Bales to London, the whole town is employ'd in
spinning, weaveing, washing, trying and dressing their Bayes, in which they seem very
industrious.' Norwich has, as well as a ca-
thedral, '3 Hospitalls for boys girls and old
people who spinn yarne, as does all the town
besides for the Crapes, Callimanco [Calico] and
Damaskes which is the whole business of the
place. Indeed they are arrived to a great perfec-
tion in their worke so fine and thinn and glossy

their pieces are 27 yards in length and their price is from 50 shillings to three pound as they are in fineness; a man can weave 13 yards a day, I saw some weaving, they are all employ'd in spinning, knitting weaveing dying scouring fulling or bleaching their stuffs.'

Exeter is 'a town very well built the streets are well pitch'd spacious noble streets and a vast trade is carryd on; as Norwich is for crapes callimanco and damaske soe this is for Serges – there is an incredible quantety of them made and sold in the town; their market day is Fryday which supplys with all things like a faire almoste; ... the whole town and country is employ'd for at least 20 miles round in spinning, weaveing, dressing and scouring, fulling and drying of the serges, it turns the most money a weeke of anything in England ...'

At Taunton there is an unusual dress note: 'You meete all sorts of country women wrapp'd up in the mantles called West Country rockets [rochets], a large mantle doubled together of a sort of serge, some are linseywolsey, and a deep fringe or fag at the lower end; these hang down some to their feets some only just below the wast, in the summer they ar all in white garments of this sort, in the winter they are in red ones ... they never go out without them and this is the universal fashion in Sommerset and Devonshire and Cornwall.' This kind of local dress rarely gets recorded.

The only other specific reference to a garment is in her note about Kendal: 'The Kendall Cotton is used for blanckets and the Scotts use them for their plodds [plaids] and there is much made here and also linsiwoolseys ... twice a weekes the market furnished with all sorts of things.' Kendal Cottons were woollen cloth generally dyed green, a reminder of Falstaff's 'three misbegotten knaves in Kendal green'.

The Importance of Appearances

The sheer toil, trouble and frustrations involved in dress in the centuries when everything, from spinning and weaving the cloth to cutting out the garment and the last stitch of the last seam had to be done by hand, are difficult to appreci-

ate in our age of mechanization and mass-production.

Many hands, toiling industriously, may have made light work of dress problems for the very rich, but they would make light pockets for the majority of people, and clothes were costly, a major item of expenditure for all who had any regard for appearances. They had to be cherished and made to last. They were refurbished, altered, given new trimmings of lace, ribbon, frilling, brought up to date, eventually often cut down for a smaller member of the family. Such expedients were resorted to by all classes of society, including the apparently prosperous.

In *The Lives of the Norths*, which throws much light upon seventeenth-century life and habits, Roger North describes his visits to Sir Dudley North: 'I have come there [to his house] and found him very busy in picking out the stitches of a displaced petticoat', prior to a renovation carried out by his wife. Elizabeth Pepys was housebound for a whole day doing a similar refurbishing; the diarist notes: 'So home, and dined with my wife, who, poor wretch, sat undressed all day till ten at night, altering and lacing of a noble petticoat.'

Nearly all classes found clothes a constant problem, usually because of the high cost and

11 A family group, early seventeenth century, from an illustration for the Roxburghe Ballads.

the time and trouble it took to get garments made and then the trouble of caring for them and keeping them in good condition. Only the very wealthy, who could command ample services for making and maintaining, and the poor, who would aim at little more than home-made, handed-down or charity coverings, were immune from these problems.

The *Memoirs of the Verney Family*, a matchless source of information on family life in the main part of the seventeenth century, is nowhere more revealing than in the letters in which younger members of the family appeal for parental help over their wardrobes. The Verneys were of some note, long-established 'landed gentry' with a history of public service at times, but here they are private people with everyday clothes problems that could be acute and distressing; it is as ordinary people that their chronicler, Lady Verney (who was Florence Nightingale's elder sister), saw her forebears. It was after her marriage to Sir Harry Verney in 1858 that she started editing the vast collection of 30,000 letters which had lain forgotten in boxes in a gallery at the top of the family house, Claydon, in Buckinghamshire, some of them going back to Henry VII's time, but extending to 1696. 'Most of the work of the world is done by average men and women,' she suggests.

The younger men of the family, dependent upon their parents, have many clothes problems. Thus Tom Verney in 1638 writes to Sir Ralph, his father, with many requests. He has 'hardly any clothes left, neither bands, ruffs, shirts, boothose, boots, or anything else but is upon my back'. He is rescued: subsequently a tailor 'charges for a grey cloth suit for Mr Thomas Verney' and 'for a collar, and callyco to lyne and stitch a tafety doublet'. Later Tom asks for 'three small parcells of things, and then I will not trouble you noe more this three months – two paire of gloves, two paire of linen stockings, two paire of plaine boothose topps, two paire of woollen boothose and three handkerchiefs. A very small matter buys them.'

About the middle of the seventeenth century letters between Sir Ralph and his wife Mary deal with clothes. He quizzes her about not having worn her new clothes: 'Sure you meane to sell them and bring mee a minte of money, or else the vanitie of others hath abated your pride ... Certainly we are much of a humour at this time about our cloathes, for did you but see how I am patched upp with old frippery, you could not but admire it; but I deferre all my bravery till you come.' That there was no social stigma in selling one's clothes secondhand and that shabbiness was no ignomiy are facts that recur in records of this time. Thus in 1650 Sir Ralph's friend, Sir Henry Newton, writes from Paris about an old coat which Sir Ralph had asked him to sell for him: it is difficult to get a good price for it as 'the moths have been very busie with it.'

Mun, as Edmund, another of Ralph's sons, was known, writes from The Hague for 150 yards of black ribbon to trim a grey and black cloth doublet to be worn with scarlet silk stockings, which will make proper attire, or black if his father prefers. He also needs some Cordova gloves. Sir Ralph thinks 150 yards excessive for bows; 'soe a suit be whole, cleane, and fashionable I care not how plaine it bee'.

Mun's brother John is, in contrast, careful over his wardrobe. He chooses with care: 'Mr Denton the Taylour hath brought mee a sute of closes of same Cloth that my Cloke is off; he hath also brought mee a sote with a pair of upper stokings, and a pair of under reade stockings.' He has, however, a few smaller wants: 'I doe lake some blacke rubin for to make mee some cuffestrings and shoostrings against christmas ... I doe allso take a hatt against christmas, for my oulde hat which I have now is full of holes in the croune of it.'

In 1662 John Verney, who has been apprenticed to a textile trader in London (a significant sign of changing social standards) is going overseas for a 12-year post with a firm of textile exporters and his wardrobe is listed. He takes with him clothes which cost £50 in all, including 'Holland for caps, handkerchiefs, and doublets £1.7.0, lace for the caps 4s 9d, cloth for two pair of socks 3s 0d, six pair thread stirrup stockings 10s 0d, two pair white stockings £2, six pair of Shoes and one pair Slippers £1.9.10, seven pair gloves 9s 0d, Tailor's bill for £16.10.0.'

His employers are stated to have as their main exports 'Cotton and Cotton Wools, Galls for Dyers, Aniseeds, Cordovants, Wax, Grosgram, Yarns, Chamlets ... Mohairs and Raw Silks brought overland from Persia, and Goatshair.' To offset this, 'the Company's ships brought back in return the famous English cloth from Suffolk, Essex and Gloucester; kerseys from Yorkshire and Hampshire ...'.

In 1685 Edmund's son, also Edmund, is 16

12 *'A Merry New Song' from Tempest's* Cries of London *(1688–1702)*.

and going to Oxford. His father sends off his trunk of clothes after him, including everything 'except yr old Camelote coate, wch I Didd not think you would need nor worth sending; yr old Hatt I Didd not send neither, for it was soe Badd that I was ashamed of it.'

The Verney ladies, like their menfolk, could at times feel shabby compared with other women, and this was particularly galling when they were outshone by those of a lower rank. Thus 'the silk gowns of the Miss Berts excited the envy of the better-born and much worse-dressed Miss Verneys.' Again, Jack Verney, as an apprentice, is staying with his employers, the Roberts, and is visited by his aunt Penelope. Says the memoir: 'If Mrs Gabriel Roberts and her daughters craned their necks out of the window to see the young apprentice's fashionable relations, they probably derived some feminine satisfactions in contrasting the shabbiness of Aunt Penelope's attire with their own rich silk gowns and riding-hoods, for the worthy merchant was prospering greatly.'

There is also a Verney description of the informal morning attire of women of the time: 'I found Mrs Mary in her morning dress, a white and blacke petty cote and wast coate, and all cleane and fine linnen, so lovely proper and briske I protest I knewe her not at first sight.'

A Ballad View of Dress

A more cheerful view of dress is given in the *Roxburghe Ballards*, that 'collection of Ancient Songs and Ballards, written on various subjects, and printed between the years MDLX and MDCC'. Such folk literature reveals much about contemporary attitudes.

The tailor was clearly very much part of the community, frequently mentioned. There is the ballad which runs:

> There was a Lass had three Lovers,
>   The one of them a Taylor,
> The second waas a monied man,
>   The third a Joviall Saylor;

The Taylor gave his Love a Gowne,
    In love and kinde good will;
The Usurer, with his money bags,
    Her purse did often fill.

The happy simplicity of the country girl comes in for frequent praise in the ballads, as in one in which she is the speaker:

> Although I am a Country Lasse,
>   A loftie mind I beare a,
> I think my self as good as those,
>   That gay apparel weare a.
>
> My coate is made of comely Gray,
>   Yet is my skin as soft a,
> As those that with the chiefest Wines,
>   Do bathe their bodies oft a.

Again, the girl voices her contentment with her humble lot:

> I care not to weare Gallant raggs,
>   And owe the Taylour for them,
> I care not for those vaunting brags,
>   I ever did abhor them.

Fortunately, she is wooed for her simplicity. Says the man who adores her:

> A country Lasse in russet gray,
>   With her I love to sport and play,
> O she will dance, and sweetly sing,
>   Much like the Nightingale in Spring.

But another girl from Worcestershire is tempted by London and its luxury, with gifts from many admirers.

> One gives to me perfumed Gloves,
>   The best that he can buy me . . .
> If any new toyes I will have,
>   I have them, cost they ne're so deare, –
>
> My fashions with the Moone I change,
>   As though I were a Lady;
> All quaint conceits, both new and strange,
>   Ile have as soon as may be.

The present luxury of young men's lace and ruffles is compared with the good old days when

13 *Spinning out of doors, an illustration for the Roxburghe Ballads.*

> Their fathers went in homely frees,
>   And good plain broad cloathes breeches,
> Their stockings with the same agrees,
>   Sow'd on with good strong stitches.

3
Moving with the Times

A Suit for All

With the end of the Civil War the Restoration marked the start of a period of expansion and development affecting every aspect of life and every class of the populace, to an extent never seen before. Men sailed the seas as explorers and merchant adventurers, spurred on by the twin excitements of new-found lands and new trade markets which would bring power and wealth to the country and to the individual. The great sweep of science and invention, which was to transform the world, found a springboard in the founding of the Royal Society in London in 1660, and in 1662 it received its Royal Charter and the active support of Charles II and Prince Rupert, both of whom were keen amateur scientists. The Bank of England was established in 1690 and this gave business a boost.

Social changes were implicit in these events and men's dress, which still dominated the clothes scene, as it had done in the past, reflected this because men's way of life was changing. The former richness and extravagance of fashionable attire, the doublets and trunk hose, the bombasted splendour, the great ruffs and feathers, the fanciful accoutrements of Elizabethan times had no place in a world where activity and achievement involved all classes and where class barriers were breaking down. The ordinary man counted for much more – and there were more of him to count. What James Laver called 'a real revolution in male attire' took place – and that meant in all male attire.

By about 1620 all classes were wearing breeches similar to what ordinary men had been wearing for centuries in most countries. Some kind of jacket, also everyday dress for centuries,

began to be fashionable wear too. A third garment, a long waistcoat which might be seen as an adaptation of some of the previous elaborate male garments, was added and the trio, known as a 'suit', was worn by all classes.

This name was not new. In *The Male Image* Penelope Byrde records that 'in the fourteenth century the Great Wardrobe accounts of Edward III listed "suits of clothes" of three, four, five or six garments each, and the term continued in use during the next three centuries.' Samuel Pepys referred to his 'suits' both before and after the period when the coat, waistcoat and knee breeches came into fashion. On 3 September 1665, the year of the Great Fire, he wrote: 'Up and put on my coloured silk suit, very fine.'

Both John Evelyn and Samuel Pepys have recorded how this change in men's dress to what in numerous forms has been the basic outfit of all classes ever since took place, and how it started off with a Royal accolade. Evelyn, for once, steals some of the thunder from his more dress-conscious contemporary and claims to have had some share in contriving a style of dress which is generally believed to have been introduced into Court circles by Charles II. He records that in October 1666 the doublet and trunk hose then still in vogue in high society were bringing their wearers into general disrepute because they were a French mode. England was at war with France. He claims that he suggested their replacement by 'a comely vest, after the Persian mode'. He continues with an invective against current fashions for men. This attack he gave to the King to read. On 18 October he writes in his diary: 'To

London to our office, and now I had on the vest and surcoat or tunic as 'twas called, after His Majesty had brought the whole Court to it. It was a comely and manly habit, too good to hold.'

Pepys mentions the King's new clothes on 13 October, when he says he visited the Duke of York, the King's brother, later James II, and '...so I stood and saw him dress himself and try on his vest, which is the king's new fashion and he will be in it for good and all on Monday next, and the whole court; it is a fashion, the king says, he will never change'. Two days later on 15 October, he writes: 'This day the King begins to put on his vest, and I did see several persons of the House of Lords and Commons too, great courtiers who are in it; being a long cassock close to the body, of black cloth, and pinked with white silke under it, and a coat over it, and the legs ruffled with black riband like a pidgeon's leg, and upon the whole I wish the King may keep it, for it is a very fine and handsome garment.'

By November Pepys had followed the Royal lead and he writes: 'My taylor's man brings my vest home, and coat to wear with it ... I rose and dressed myself, and like myself mightily in it, and so do my wife ... it being very cold, to Whitehall, and was mightily fearfull of an ague, my vest being new and thin, and the coat cut not to meet before, upon my vest.'

The man's suit, which is what the new outfit amounted to, had come to stay. It could be interpreted in ways appropriate to all classes and needs. It also gave a great impetus to the adoption of wool for men's dress, instead of the silks, brocades and velvets which had previously been favoured by high fashion. Charles is said to have been one of the first men of fashion to show a strong preference for wool. The suit would encourage this, being a big step towards more practical dressing and capable of adoption by all classes.

The suit also influenced the course of dress because it encouraged the craft of the tailor. 'By 1680,' says Phillis Cunnington, 'experiments in better cut and fit were being attempted, made possible by the wider use of woollen cloth by all classes'. Such cloth could be shaped and handled with a precision not possible in the case of silks and velvets of widely variable textures and weaves. The woollen suit had indeed come to stay – from then until now. Long straight coats were the first choice in the last quarter of the seventeenth century. The 'vest' was the later 'waistcoat' and at that time it was usually as long as the coat or even longer. At first both were straight, but by the end of the century the

14 *The Little Man, at St Alban's Abbey: a simple version of the seventeenth-century suit.*

coat was in the more familiar, waisted, full-skirted style, often worn open to show the vest and shirt underneath. Breeches, worn for centuries by working men in town and country, were now worn generally in all classes until the beginning of the nineteenth century.

For the student of dress there is an odd footnote to this seventeenth-century move towards more democratic dress in the shape of a reference to the duffel coat. In 1683 William Byrde of Virginia grumbled: 'The duffel is the worst I ever saw ... colour too light, a darker blue pleases better.' In the next century Defoe says that duffel, 'a coarse woollen stuff', was exported to the New World, but was also 'much worn here in winter'.

Restoration Women More at Ease

Women's dress followed a similar trend to that of men as regards an underlying practicality, a general adoption of a style more capable of being worn by ordinary people than was the Elizabethan farthingale. The farthingale had continued to be a fashion well into the early years of the seventeenth century, even though it was eminently for the leisured and extravagant, impossible for those with any commitment to physical or other activities – or for anyone's ordinary life.

Though the farthingale is almost exclusively shown as the dress of Elizabethan women, there was, and continued to be alongside future extreme fashions, an alternative already widely worn, the mode known as 'undress'. It was much less formal and consisted at this time of a long, full but unstiffened skirt and a separate bodice, an almost timeless mode of attire worn by all women, though capable of a great range of variety in fabric and detail. The seventeenth-century skirt was known as the 'petticoat', a

15 *A seventeenth-century Old Clothes Man, from Tempest's* Cries of London, *1688–1702; a suit similar to that in the previous illustration, but showing more detail, flapping coat, baggy breeches and a very long waistcoat.*

word which then and long afterwards normally meant an outer garment. That is what Pepys meant when he spoke of buying his wife a petticoat, and Jane Austen was still using the word in the same sense. In the seventeenth century it could be plain or highly decorative, as references by Pepys show.

The top at that time was usually a waistcoat. It was fitted to the waist and usually extended a few inches below it. It was long-sleeved, buttoned up the front, with or without a collar, and was normally made by the tailor, who was still almost the only maker of fitted clothing. Such was the waistcoat referred to by Sarah Fell in her accounts.

A seventeenth-century description of a petticoat calls it 'the skirt of a gown without its body ... worn either under a gown, or without it.' It was in fact the outer garment worn by most women and it was chiefly made by the wearer herself or by the sempstress, who was beginning to gain ground as a maker of women's dress.

It has already been said that up to the end of the seventeenth century men tailors made most of women's outer garments, as well as those of men, mainly because the elaborate shaping required for clothes up to then called for the skill of which only men who had served their apprenticeship in a long-established craft were capable. Even women of modest means and tastes used such tailors, as witness Sarah Fell's many references to her local tailor.

In spite of their expertise in needlework there is little evidence of ordinary women making main garments for themselves and their families, and to do so would have been an onerous addition to the large amount of general sewing called for from the housewife. But after the seventeenth century women did emerge who undertook sewing as a job, to make money they needed by the exercise of the only skill many of them possessed. They took over more and more of the making of clothes for their own sex.

They were known as 'mantua-makers' until well into the nineteenth century; the mantua was one of the 'undress' garments gaining in general popularity from the Restoration period. It was a loose, one-piece gown, wrapped over in front, and therefore easily made by one woman dressmaker. Materials ranged from rich silk for the wealthy to the rough woollens of the labouring classes, with finer woollens in between for the busy middle class, steadily growing in numbers.

The term 'nightgown', like 'petticoat', had in the seventeenth century and long afterwards a different meaning from that of later times. If this was not so what could be made of the account by Lady Anne Clifford in her diary of 1617 that she 'went to church in my rich nightgown and petticoat'? It usually meant an evening or other rather special gown and continued to do so for a long time. In 1784 Georgiana, the beautiful Duchess of Devonshire, 'went to the Ball. I had an English nightgown of muslin with small silver sprigs and all white'. When the actual nightgown, which started as a kirtle or shift, the basic daytime item of underwear for all classes, attained its own identity it was called a bedgown by both sexes. But even then a certain vagueness remained, because that word was also at times applied to what would later be called a dressing gown.

One item of underwear and a very important one fell into a category of its own and was worn through most of history by most women who considered their appearance, unless they were of the very poor. It was the corset. Though predominantly a woman's garment, versions of it were also to some considerable extent worn by men at various periods, mainly those of elaborate dress, such as Elizabethan days and to some degree a significant part of the seventeenth century, when the first suits were very elaborate affairs indeed.

The corset was known as the 'stays' until the nineteenth century. It was important to women's dress at most periods and never more so than in the later seventeenth century. Dress then might be more relaxed, with separate bodices or waistcoats and petticoats, but these were unstiffened, unlike the rigid Elizabethan farthingales and bodices which were provided with their own built-in supporting frameworks of whalebone, metal or wood. Henceforth the stays became a separate item of dress, usually a whaleboned rigid tube, extending probably from under the armpits to below the waist.

Stays were almost always made by a male staymaker from very early times to the seventeenth and eighteenth centuries, though latterly a few women also went into the business. The reason probably was that the craft of the tailor was needed to shape the intricate 'cage' to the shape of the wearer's body or to effect an improvement on Nature in this respect at a time when pattern-making was a matter of special skill. It was, however, suggested by R. Campbell in his *Complete English Tradesman* (1747) that one reason for the continued male near-monopoly was that fitting stays to the wearer was a feat of strength beyond the capacity of the mantua-maker, the woman dressmaker who by then had taken over the greater part of the feminine wardrobe, except for the strictly tailored coat, cloak and riding habit – which to the present day are often made by a male tailor.

About the middle of the seventeenth century the dress of the ordinary woman was recorded for the first time with devoted care and meticulous detail for its own sake. Hitherto such attention had rarely been given to anything except the fashionable attire of royal and aristocratic ladies in portraits painted by leading artists of the times. The innovation came from the Czech engraver, Wenceslas Hollar, best known for his detailed recording of London scenes and London buildings of the years before the Great Fire, but also the first to depict contemporary women with equal precision and superb skill in several series of engravings which continued to be reprinted for many years after they first appeared. The subjects included the high-born and the obscure, Court ladies, townswomen and countrywomen. The engravings were the precursors of fashion plates, but in themselves not fashion plates. In some respects they are more, because of the meticulous attention given to every detail of the dress and accessories and because of the realistic style, free from the topical exaggerations of the pure fashion drawing.

Hollar, born in Prague in 1607, came to London in the late 1630s, having already made his name as an etcher and illustrator of repute in Germany, after fleeing there from the Thirty Years War in his native country. His *Ornatus Muliebris Anglicanus* of 1640, his first English publication, showed 26 pictures of English-women and carried the sub-title, 'The Several Habits of English Women from the Nobility to the Countrywoman as They are in these Times'. They are small prints, about six inches high. Next came *Theatrum Mulierum* in 1643, 36 prints of the women of Europe, later expanded to 100 prints under the title *Aula Veneris* (1650). All these too are small and are believed to be portraits of real women. The larger engravings, known as *The Four Seasons*, exist in two forms showing three-quarter-length and full-length figures of four women, their dress shown with great intricacy. The full-length series was published in 1643, after the other, but both continued to be reprinted for many years. They show well-dressed ladies but are realistic enough to be of general value as representing dress of the time. From then onwards more attention came to be given to the portrayal of dress for its own sake, though later in life Hollar did not return to it as a subject and he had no immediate successors.

Various other sources contribute to knowledge of ordinary clothes of the late seventeenth century. Inventories are given in wills preserved in different parts of the country and can be revealing. Typical probably is that of a humble woman who left three gowns, five petticoats, skirts, a 'safeguard' (an apron or overall), a cloak, three hats, three waistcoats and 'wearing linen' (presumably underwear) with some accessories. Women, according to wills, usually left larger wardrobes than men of the same class. Men of the humbler sort seem usually to have had a doublet or vest, a hat, leather and woollen breeches, a jerkin (informal

16 *A Scottish woman by Hollar, from* Ornatus Muliebris Anglicanus, *1640.*

29

R. Gaywood fecit   3

jacket), two or three shirts, several 'bands' for the neck, and two pairs of shoes.

While the clothing of the poor was largely rudimentary and static from Restoration times, that of the rising middle classes was becoming more varied and more fully recorded. It centred upon London, which was very much on the up and up. The population grew from half-a-million to between three-quarters and a million in the second half of the seventeenth century. Shops abounded and increased; country people as well as Londoners used them on visits or by sending for goods to be conveyed to them by coach or through visiting friends. The shops remained small – usually the ground floor of a house was turned into a shop by means of a window let down to show an array of the growing variety of goods on offer. But they boasted displays and variety as no other town did. Glass windows also began to appear. The shopkeeper, his wife and family would all help in the shop, but could also move upstairs and lived under the same roof. This continued through the eighteenth century and was probably the origin of the living-in system for shop employees in the nineteenth. London as a place for acquiring clothes was far ahead of anywhere else, even though accounts vary. John Evelyn complains of the dirt, especially of the 'horrid smoke from coal which ... foules our clothes', and of the stenches made by breweries, soap boilers and dyers. But Pepys decked himself out in a summer suit of coloured camelot, with a flowered tabby vest and gold lace sleeves, and his clothes in general, like those of his wife, were colourful and gay. London shops sold a host of small items which could tempt shoppers of many types, which meant almost all who could afford to make any purchases. Goods ranged from scarves, shawls, gloves, stockings, caps, hats and lace to trimmings galore and above all

17 *Seventeenth-century simplicity in a dark dress and hood, with white collar, cuffs and apron, by Richard Gaywood, after Hollar's 'Autumne' from* The Four Seasons; *1656.*

the ribbons which Restoration men as well as women delighted in decking their clothes with at every point from head to toe. A stroll along one of the popular shopping centres, like the New Exchange in the Strand, was a happy diversion and a popular one.

Probably the greatest perennial attraction of Samuel Pepys is that he is the first literary man with whom we feel that we chat, compare notes and are on easy, neighbourly, gossipy terms as he goes about his daily affairs. He is the ordinary middle-class man. With him we share the everyday enjoyments and irritations, pleasures and frustrations that make the passing day. Especially this is so when we go shopping with him, stand at his elbow as he organizes some item of his own wardrobe or that of his Elizabeth. The former takes priority on many occasions; not only is he the son of a tailor, but his position as Clerk of the Acts at the Navy Office requires, as he points out, that he shall be well dressed.

Thus he goes shopping and orders clothes from his tailor, attending carefully to everything and usually enjoying doing so: the modern man. In detail he records: 'And so to Sir W. Turner's, and there bought my cloth, coloured, for a suit and cloake, to line with plush the cloakes, which will cost me money. But I find I must go handsomely, what ever it cost me, and the charge will be made up in the fruit it brings.'

He makes a joint purchase when, in 1668, he 'laid out four pounds in lace, for her and me.' On 15 April, 1661 he records that he went 'with my wife, by coach, to the New Exchange, to buy her some things, where we saw some new fashion pety-coats of sarcenett [a kind of silk] with a broad lace printed round the bottom and before, very handsome, and my wife has a mind to some of them'. On 22 June 1661, he tells that 'the day before, my wife put on her slashed waistcoate, which is very pretty'. On 29 June of the same year: 'To church with my wife, who this day put on her green petticoate of flowered satten, with fine white and black gimp lace of her own putting on, which is very pretty.' On 25 June there is another note: 'She by my Lady's advice desires a new petticoat of the new silk striped stuff very pretty. So I went to Pater Noster Row presently, and bought her a very fine rich one – the best I did see there, and much better than she desires or expects.' There was a grand occasion in 1664 when: 'She has put on her new best gown, which indeed is very fine now with the lace, and this morning her taylor brought home her other new laced silk gown with a smaller lace, and new petticoat I bought the other day: both very pretty.'

A year or two later there is another new outfit: 'My wife having dressed herself in a silky dress of a blue petticoat uppermost, and white satin waistcoat and white hood, though I think she did it because her gown is gone to the tailor's, did, together with me being hungry, which always makes me peevish, make me angry.'

More trouble over a petticoat when: 'I to bed, and left my wife to do something to a waistband and a petticoat she is to wear tomorrow.' In contrast in May 1669 he records: 'My wife extraordinary fine with her flowered tabby gown.' Tabby was watered silk, fashionable at that time.

Pepys shares the current trend towards the wearing of woollen cloth, rather than silks and velvets. Thus in 1679 he records, 'that I did resolve of putting me into a better garbe; and among other things, to have a good velvet cloak, that is, of cloth lined with velvet.'

Even he is not above making a purchase of a secondhand garment. On one occasion in 1662, 'I walked to my brother Tome to see a velvet cloake, which I buy of Mr Moore; it will cost me 8/- 10s – but it is worth my money.'

He describes an occasion when he feels particularly well-turned out: 'This morning I put on my best black-cloth suit trimmed with Scarlet ribbon, very neat, with my cloak lined with Velvet and a new Beaver, which altogether is very noble, with my black silk canons I bought a month ago.' He refers to a nightgown and night cap more than once, but, as would be expected, does not use the word in today's sense – one such mention occurs when the Deputy Governor of the Tower sends for his 'nightgown of silk, only to make a show to use'.

Wigs for Men

Changes in the man's suit continued to be made, mainly in the direction of simplification and eliminating the first cumbersome and elaborate Restoration versions, but the three-piece – jacket or coat, waistcoat or vest and breeches, later trousers – remained the basis of male dress from then until the present day. Only the very poor, who could not afford the suit, failed to wear it in some form. In town and country, from landed gentry and men of business or affairs to shopkeepers and farm workers there was no substitute for the suit, though, of course, the materials as well as the styling varied immensely. Fine broadcloths were for the prosperous. Working men, and countrymen in particular, usually had rougher versions of breeches – of leather or coarse woollens – and less shapely jerkins for everyday wear.

In the face of this simplification, which was appropriate to forward-looking attitudes and a loosening of class distinction, it is difficult to account for a startling innovation in dress which swept through all classes of men at almost the same time as the introduction of the suit. This was the wig, or to be exact, the periwig. It was not a passing fashion, because the wig was worn in various forms by all classes for more than a century. It seemed to contradict any theory that men's dress was becoming more rational. It baffled James Laver, who described it as 'Perhaps the most extraordinary event that has ever happened in the history of male costume'. It was not, as later, a substitute for natural hair, nor an accessory, but an article of dress in its own right.

The reason for the adoption of the wig has never been satisfactorily explained. During the seventeenth century men's hair had been worn longer and longer among the fashionable, elaborately arranged and waved and curled. This must have been a laborious and continuous operation, because few of the effects were natural, and for those men with poor hair or

18 *A Big-Wig to the fore in a cartoon of 1752, showing a crowd outside Whitehall Chapel, sold as a print by a Ludgate Hill shop. Other wigs in various styles can also be seen.*

bald heads there must have been much embarrassment. At the same time ordinary men's natural hair was cut to various lengths in a conventional way.

One widespread belief is that the wearing of periwigs started with Louis XIII of France, said to have worn a wig when he went bald because he felt that his prestige and dignity as king at the head of a nation already famed as a fashion leader were threatened. But that was in 1624, and travellers in France had seen *perruques* (translated as 'periwigs'), some time before that.

In England Pepys records the adoption of the wig. He states in his diary on 3 November 1663 that the Duke of York has said that he intends to wear a periwig and that the king, his brother, is rumoured to plan likewise. Prior to that, however, Pepys had already referred in some detail to the wearing of the periwig and to his own resistance to the idea of adopting it, although many men were beginning to do so. It appeared to him that it would raise as many problems as it would solve.

On 9 May 1663 he put the case for and against wigs: 'At Mr Jarvas's my old barber, I did try two or three borders and periwigs, meaning to wear one, and yet I have no stomach for it, but that the pains of keeping my hair clean is so great. He trimmed me, and at last I parted, but my mind was almost altered from my first purpose, from the trouble that I foresee will be in wearing them also.' In August he discusses

33

the problem with his brother Tom, who works with their father, the tailor, and succumbs to fashion. 'We did resolve of putting me into a better garbe . . . and a perruque.' On 30 August, smartened up by a new velvet cloak which he had ordered ('that is, lined with velvet, a good cloth the outside'), he took his wife to his periwig maker's to see the new periwig, 'which she said she liked.' He bought two, along with a variety of other clothing, and that night added up the bills recording that one had cost £3, the other £2.

With royalty confirming his decision on 2 November Pepys saw his periwig-maker on the next day and 'without more ado I went up and there he cut off my haire, which went a little to my heart at present to part with it, but, it being over, and my periwig on, I paid him £3 for it, and away went he, with my own haire, to make up another of'. He felt some embarrassment at appearing in his wig before his friends, but the wearing of wigs spread rapidly to all classes and lasted for more than a century.

A wig which went off to the periwig-maker or barber to be cared for was a tempting acquisition. It may also be that men felt a desire to counteract the new, much simpler fashion of a suit by doing something about their crowning glory.

The wig at first followed the natural lines of the hair, and was made in natural hair colourings, from blond to black. But by about 1680 as a fashion it had become huge and elaborate, described as 'full-bottomed', and had a mass of curls and waves, intricately arranged and sometimes sweeping over the shoulders and down the back as far as the waist. Prices could be very high, as much as fifty guineas. Originally human hair was used, but as the demand soared and all classes took to wearing wigs, horse hair and goat hair and even wool were used for cheaper versions. Pepys recorded an alarming rumour that during the Plague Year of 1665 the hair of people who had died of the disease was being used to make wigs, with a resulting spread of the infection.

19 *Wigs of many styles featured in a London print of 1773.*

By the beginning of the eighteenth century many variations in wig styles were being worn, including shorter, tied-back ones for travel, sport and for working men. These were very widely worn by ordinary people. Agricultural labourers are recorded as wearing them. Prices therefore had to cover all levels. They had various names, including the bob, the ramillie, the pig-tail, the cadogan, the campaigne and the bag-wig. For years wigs were the chief point of interest in masculine dress, to a large extent replacing hats as decorative items of attire.

The powdered wig was introduced about 1710, the powder being either grey or white. It became popular. The powder closet was introduced in honour of the wig, because the powdering process could create an alarming amount of dust from the starch or flour usually employed.

20 *A barber's shop, 1771, showing:* a. *barber at work;* b. *arranging a wig;* c. *heating curling tongs:* d. *customer wiping powder off face.*

The wig solved the problems of hair-washing, not too frequently done according to the habits of the time. But the wig did not deal with the problem of hair care; it needed constant professional attention to keep it in trim, and that cost money. No doubt when worn by the poorer classes, as it very generally was, it was not immaculate, and it was often among the items offered in secondhand shops.

Dr Johnson, whose neglect of his appearance was the concern of many of his friends, had particular trouble with his wig. After meeting the Thrales through a mutual friend, Arthur Murphy, he was invited to dinner with them and was soon dining there on Thursdays and then even more frequently. He was not the perfect guest; he seldom changed his linen, or washed himself, would use a book as a plate at meals and his wig, Boswell says, was a disaster: 'The great bushy wig, which throughout his life he affected to wear, by that closeness of texture which it had contracted and been suffered to retain, was ever nearly as impenetrable by a comb as a quickset hedge; and little of the dust that had once settled on his outer garments was ever known to have been disturbed by the brush.'

When Dr Johnson moved to Streatham, where he practically lived with the Thrales for 16 years, they took charge of his appearance. Henry Thrale 'saw to it that Johnson's clothes were clean and of sober good quality with silver buttons, that he wore silver buckles in his shoes ... and changed his shirt at seemly intervals. When there were visitors to dinner it was the task of a servant to stand outside the dining-room ready to provide Johnson with a company wig instead of the everyday one his poor sight had caused him to frizzle in the candle'.

There is also an illuminating paragraph in Sophie von la Roche's account of crossing the Channel to visit England in 1786. In the morning, before disembarking, all the men sat in a row wearing night caps while their barbers put their wigs in trim; while they wore slippers, their shoes were cleaned for them. Parson Woodforde was embarrassed at being 'caught on the hop, busy in my garden, and dressed in my cotton morning gown, old wigg and Hat' by an unexpected visitor.

Though more a ploy of the fashionable than of ordinary people, powder was widely enough used for it to be worth while for William Pitt, as Prime Minister, to introduce a tax on hair powder in 1798. It so enraged his political opponents that, rallied together by the Duke of Beaufort, they resolved to stop powdering their wigs, with such effect that the use of hair powder soon came to be limited to the elderly or old-fashioned. Natural hair returned to favour as the complete answer to the problem. From the end of the eighteenth century only the Court and the army used powder.

Though men's wigs were such a dramatic feature of their dress women's hair styles showed no tendency to follow suit. Simple curls and ringlets were the prevalent style among women till the end of the seventeenth century, sometimes with ribbon bows or strings of pearls as adornment for the fashionable, while ordinary women usually wore fairly plain caps or bonnets over hair that was no more than pinned up. At the beginning of the eighteenth century there was a fashion for a high headdress of lawn or lace attached to the front of the cap, with the hair coiled up below it. This was called the 'fontange' after a French duchess who wore it, or a 'commode' or 'tower'. But it never became general wear. The built-up, fabulous head-dresses of late-eighteenth-century court ladies used artificial hair as well as wire, feathers, ribbons, flowers, even stuffed birds for their freakish effects, but had no practical links either with the omnipresent wigs of men or with the very simple hairdressing of ordinary women, who were more interested in the choice of caps and hats, to which they were greatly addicted, than in elaborate hair styles.

4
Eighteenth Century Variety

Boom in the Wool Trade

What ordinary people can wear at any period depends largely on what is available and how accessible and affordable it is. The earlier part of the eighteenth century is somewhat difficult to assess today in these terms, mainly because we think of it as the end of an era, overshadowed by the on-coming sweep of the Industrial Revolution, of machines and inventions that would transform the whole pattern of life and dress for most people. However, by those living then the period was regarded as the very peak of achievement, the consummation of the past, a proud moment in history, especially for ordinary people. Travel and transport were improving dramatically, unifying the country and its people, knocking days off the time it took to get from one part of the country to another. Trade at home and overseas was booming.

This was the scene which Daniel Defoe depicted in his *A Tour Through the Whole Island of Great Britain* (1724–26), which is probably the most illuminating contemporary study of the subject. A brilliant and perceptive working journalist and a wide-ranging writer who had also had practical experience of trade, he found a dominating theme in the ebullience and rising prosperity of the woollen trade and its insatiable demand for the textiles which were still the mainstay of the home and export trade, indeed of the nation's prosperity. He found the cloth-weaving area around Halifax so riveting that he made three visits to it and wrote of it with an intensity of enthusiasm that defied wind and weather, snow and an ugly country-

21 *Traditional spinning out-of-doors in an eighteenth-century village.*

side, all uphill and downhill, and sent him into raptures.

As he neared Halifax he found 'the houses thicker, and the villages greater in every bottom, and not only so, but the sides of the hills, which were very steep every way, were spread with houses, and that very thick'. As regards the houses 'though we saw no people stirring without doors, yet they were all full within; ... those people all full of business; not a beggar, not an idle person to be seen, except here and there an alms-house, where people antient, decrepit, and past labor, might perhaps be found.'

As the explanation he continues: 'The business is the clothing trade, for the convenience of which the houses are thus scattered and spread upon the sides of the hills ... the reason is this; such has been the bounty of nature to this otherwise frightful country, that two things essential to the business, as well as to the ease of the people are found here, and that is a situation which I never saw the like of in any part of

England; and, I believe, the like is not to be seen so contrived in any part of the world, I mean coals and running water upon the tops of the highest hills. This seems to have been directed by the wise hand of Providence.'

He observes: 'At almost every house there was a tenter, and almost on every tenter a piece of cloth, or kersey, or shalloon ... from which the sun shining to us ... I thought it was the most agreeable sight that I ever saw.'

There is a brisk popular market for the finished fabrics. 'You see ten or twenty thousands value in cloth, and sometimes much more, bought and sold in little more than an hour.' In addition, for the ordinary people 'there are ... a set of travelling merchants in Leeds, who go all over England ... and to all the fairs and market towns over the whole island'.

38

Cheapside

23 *The Cloth Hall, Leeds, which so greatly impressed Defoe. Here seen later, in the early nineteenth century.*

Other buyers send their cloth to London, to shopkeepers and wholesalers, and also 'for exportation to the English colonies in America . . . as also to the Russia merchants'. Finally merchants sell to other merchants in Holland and many parts of Germany, 'and even to Vienna and Ausburgh, in the farthest provinces of Germany'.

In Norwich, too, Defoe finds the wool trade the outstanding source of activity and prosperity. There 'an eminent weaver' calculated for him that 'there were 120,000 people employed in the woollen and silk manufactures of that city only'.

Stourbridge's famous market, he declares, is 'not only the greatest in the whole nation, but in the world . . . The shops are placed in rows like streets . . . and here are all sorts of trades.'

Devon, Somerset and Cornwall also, Defoe finds, are all notable for a great variety of woollens, including 'serges, druggets, &c and several other kinds of stuffs', including, in Somerset towns, 'fine medley, or mix'd cloths, such as are usually worn in England by the better sort of people; and, also, exported in great quantities to Holland, Hamburgh, Sweden, Denmark, Spain, Italy &c'.

Moving on to Scotland, Defoe has a description of Glasgow textiles which is interesting because of the date: 'Here is a manufacture of plaiding, a stuff cross-strip'd with yellow and red, and other mixtures for the plaids or vails, which the ladies in Scotland wear, and which is a habit peculiar to the country. Here is a manufacture of muslins; and, perhaps the only manufacture of its kind in Britain, if not in Europe; and they make them so good and so fine, that great quantities of them are sent into England, and sold there at a good price.'

Defoe has more to say for wool, in *The Complete English Tradesman* (1727). 'We are the

39

24 *Cloth traders in the West Riding of Yorkshire, 1814.*

greatest trading country in the world', he declares roundly, and again: 'The manufactures of England, particularly of Wool (Cotton-Wool included) and of Silk, are the greatest, and amount to the greatest value of any single manufacture in Europe.'

From this he goes on to give details of the great number of different woollens and to point out that 'tho' all our manufactures are used and called for by almost all the people ... yet they are made and wrought in several distinct and respective Counties in Britain ... hardly any two manufactures being made in one place'. Most usefully of all, for posterity, he analyses the sources of the items in 'one ordinary suit of cloaths' for a man of any class:

If his Coat be of Woollen Cloth, he has that from Yorkshire.

The Lining is Shalloon, from Berkshire.

The Waistcoat is of Callamancoe from Norwich.

The Breeches of a strong Drugget from Devizes, Wiltshire.

The Stockings being of Yarn from Westmoreland.

The Hat is a felt from Leicester.

The Gloves of Leather from Somersetshire.

The Shoes from Northampton.

The Buttons from Macclesfield in Cheshire; or, if they are of Metal, they come from Birmingham, or Warwickshire.

His Garters from Manchester.

His Shirt of home-made Linen of Lancashire, or Scotland.

This applies regardless of where the family lives,

'for that all these manufactures must be found in all the remotest towns and counties in England'.

Just as illuminating is Defoe's inventory of the wardrobe of the man's wife, who 'being a good honest townsman's daughter, is not dressed over fine, yet she must have something decent, being new married'. The husband at this stage has been defined as 'a middling Tradesman, that is going to live in some market-town, and to open his shop there; suppose him not to deal in the manufacture, but in Grocery'. He will be dressed as above, but his suit 'a little finer . . . and so his comes out of Wiltshire, and his Stockings are, it may be, of Worsted [wool], not of Yarn [any material], and so they come from Nottingham, not Westmoreland'.

His wife is 'to have a silk gown, with all the necessaries belonging to a middling tolerable appearance', and that means:

Her Gown, a plain English Mantua-silk, manufactur'd in Spittlefields . . .
Her Under-petticoat, a piece of black Callamanca, made at Norwich; quilted at home, if she be a good housewife; but the quilting of Cotton from Manchester. . . .
Her Under-Petticoat, Flannel and Swanskin, from Salisbury and Wales.
Her Stockings from Tewkesbury, if ordinary; from Leicester, if woven . . .
Her Wrapper, or Morning-gown, a piece of Irish Linen, printed at London . . .

The ordinary middle-class woman was well turned out, as was her husband. Pre-industrial Britain was flourishing.

Details in Dress

Defoe's are the most detailed descriptions yet given of the clothes of ordinary people of that – or any previous – time, and particularly to be treasured because of the changes coming later in the century.

The dress of everyday life in the eighteenth century was becoming better recorded, partly because the improvement in transport meant that there was more communication between people of different types and classes. For example, artists show more interest in depicting scenes of everyday life – and clothes. Hogarth (1697–1764) was a pioneer here. He turned from portraiture to painting small groups and conversation pieces, the most successful of them being several versions from *The Beggar's Opera*; he concentrated on this type of painting and after a few years of further success, 'I . . . turned my thoughts to a still more novel mode, viz, painting and engraving modern moral subjects, a field not broken up in any country or any age.' These were to be treated dramatically, like his stage drawings. His success lay in selling engravings from them, depicting ordinary people.

As Hogarth wrote: 'I therefore wished to compose pictures on canvas, similar to representations on the stage, . . . I have endeavoured to treat my subjects as a dramatic writer, my pictures as my stage, and men and women my players.' The first of these was the *Harlot's Progress*, showing the downfall of a country girl at the hands of the wicked Londoners, several of whom could be recognized.

This project was highly successful, mainly due to the sale of engravings made from the paintings almost as they appeared in 1731–32. So great was the demand for copies that they were pirated, and this led to Hogarth's getting a copyright act passed in 1733. This move was a great encouragement to popular art, depicting ordinary people for display in their own homes. Hogarth continued with the series, which included the *Rake's Progress* and *Marriage à la Mode*. These English scenes remained his greatest successes, recording for the first time the everyday life of his time and the everyday appearance of the people involved in it.

One of the most complete descriptions of the dress of the village girl of the earlier eighteenth century is given in Richardson's *Pamela* (1740). When this most entertaining of his young heroines decides to return to her native village and is anxious not to create suspicions of the gay life she has been leading as a smart ladies' maid in town, she details the simple traditional

25 *A London street scene depicted by Hogarth:*
Beer Street, 1751.

26 *Popular art took a big step forward with Hogarth's scenes from everyday life. Here is one of the series* The Rake's Progress.

27 *Cloth weaving shown in another of Hogarth's scenes of ordinary life – two apprentices at their looms, representing industry and idleness, 1747.*

servant maid's clothes she will again assume, including the countrywoman's russet gown, the homespun woollen dress of grey or brown, symbol of rustic simplicity. Accordingly: 'I . . . put on my round-eared ordinary cap . . . my home-spun gown and petticoat and plain leather shoes . . . and my ordinary hose . . . A plain muslin tucker I put on, and my black silk necklace, instead of the French necklace my lady gave me, and put my earrings out of my ears. When I was quite equipped I took my straw hat in my hand, with its two blue strings, and looked in the glass, as proud as anything.' She adds a bundle of appropriately simple clothing, including 'a calico nightgown, that I used to wear o'mornings . . . a quilted calimanco

coat, two pair of stockings I bought of the pedlar, . . . and here are four other shifts, one the fellow to that I have on, another pretty good one, and the other two old fine ones, that will serve me to turn and wind with at home . . . and here are two pair of shoes. I have taken the lace off, which I will burn, and may-be will fetch me some little matter at a pinch, with an old silver buckle or two . . . here's a cotton handkerchief bought of a pedlar . . . and here are my new-bought mittens; this is my new flannel coat, the fellow to that I have on; and in the parcel pinned together are several pieces of printed calico, remnants of silk and such like – would serve for robings and facings and such-like uses.'

Such were the subterfuges by which the poor managed to clothe themselves. But as soon as she married 'Mr B.' Pamela resumed her former fine attire: 'Fine linen, silk shoes, and fine white

28 *A touch of the macabre in the idle 'prentice discovered by his master, again from Hogarth's series.*

cotton stockings, a fine quilted coat, a delicate green Mantua silk gown, and a French necklace, a laced cambric handkerchief, and clean gloves, and taking my fan, I, like a proud little hussy, looked in the glass, and thought myself a gentlewoman once more.' Class distinctions in dress there were, but they could by now be broken through, in the beginning of a long process which was to continue.

Some eighteenth-century garments had, however, a definite class connotation. One of the most important was the red cloak. Contemporary writings by travellers, paintings of the time and actual garments preserved in museums as relics of rural life show that such cloaks were very widely worn by country-women over a long period, until well into the nineteenth century, though their origin goes much further back to the fairy tale of Red Riding Hood. The red cloak became the almost universal party cloak of small girls by the first quarter of the present century. Anne Buck, who has investigated the story of the red cloak, concluded that it 'is of all garments the one which from its widespread use and long survival might be seen as a traditional garment of the English countryside.' But a cloak was the usual outdoor garment of all women of the eighteenth century, in various guises. Because it was so protective the hooded style came to be called the 'riding hood'. Cloaks, however, were made in almost all variations of style, hooded and hoodless, long and short, usually full-skirted, the hood often large enough to go over a scarf or hat. Red was a favourite colour, but not universal; blue and grey also appeared at times and

29 Match Girl, *1823, from a series of hand-coloured engravings entitled* England, *published in 1813 by Murray. She has a blue skirt, white apron and the red cloak so frequently worn.*

30 *A fuller, longer red cloak is worn by* Market Woman, *in the same collection as the previous illustration.*

plaid in Scotland. The red hooded cloak seems, however, to have remained almost wholly a rather humble country garment ... until those Victorian and Edwardian little girls of the middle classes made it part of their party outfits.

The red cloak perhaps steps up a little socially when described by Mary Russell Mitford in *Our Village* in the 1820s. When children flock out on a frosty winter day to slide on a frozen pond the crowd includes 'girls in red cloaks'. The writer tells the story of Red Riding Hood to a visiting little girl as a bedtime story. At the other extreme of age is her Mrs Sally Mearing, a venerable 'farmeress', also 'that good relique of the olden time ... with the hood of her red cloak pulled over her close black bonnet, of that silk which once (it may be presumed) was fashionable ... and her whole stout figure huddled up in

a miscellaneous and most substantial covering of thick petticoats, gown, aprons, shawls and cloaks'. Again, a party of gypsies met on a walk includes 'an old crone, in a tattered red cloak and black bonnet'. A fortune teller wears a 'stained, tattered cloak', also red.

The smock, generally thought of as almost the working uniform of the traditional English countryman or 'rustic' from time immemorial, has in fact a much shorter history and belongs mainly to the period from the mid-eighteenth century to towards the end of the nineteenth. Before that, rough loose overall-like garments were worn for work with horses and for farm and other chores which called for protection for the clothes, but the recognizable 'round smock'

31 *Dorsetshire peasants, wearing smocks, a long-lasting style of dress.*

was a later use of a word which had in early days been used for the basic undergarment of men and also, often, of women.

The smock, indeed, needed the advent of cheap, readily available material to become a practical garment, and that dates its rise to that of cotton in the latter part of the eighteenth century. It did, however, spread widely and became the general wear of the rural worker.

In George Eliot's *Adam Bede* (1859) the villagers are all dressed in their best for church. 'Alick, the shepherd, in his new smock-frock, taking an uneasy siesta' in the farmyard is noted.

Sometimes smocks were coloured, worn over the ordinary clothes, slipped over the head, with a neck opening, full front and back and full sleeves. The nature of the work influenced the material and colour. Some references comment admiringly on the spotless white smock frocks, but they could also be of brown, blue or other colours. The famous 'smocking' and similar embroidery belonged mainly to the garment when, in the nineteenth century, it became more general countrymen's wear, with special ones for church on Sundays. These could be made of very fine linen. The wearing of the smock began in the south of England and spread from there; eventually they were worn all over the country. Straw hats could accompany them.

Miss Mitford's *Our Village*, which is a compendium of lore about all things rural, has several references to smock frocks. In a detailed description of Joel Brent, 'the finest young man in our village' and 'a very picturesque person, just such a one as a painter would select for the background of some English landscape, where nature is shown in all her loveliness', she decries all idea of his wearing 'that wretched piece of deformity a coat, or that still wretcheder apology for a coat, a dock-tailed jacket'. He normally wears as upper garment, 'that prettier jacket without skirts – call it for the more grace a doublet', – of dark velveteen. But 'sometimes in cold weather he throws over all a smock-frock and last winter brought up a fashion ... by

assuming one of that light blue Waterloo, such as butchers wear'.

But other wearers of the garment are legion, says Miss Mitford: 'If woman be a mutable creature, man is not. The wearers of smock-frocks, in spite of the sameness of the uniform, are almost as easily distinguished ... as a flock of sheep by a shepherd ... they are in nothing new-fangled.' Joel appears again, recognizable because 'all the world knew that he wore some frocks and jackets'.

Women did not have any working garment quite comparable to the man's smock as an all-occasion cover-up, but throughout dress history they have worn aprons of every kind on many occasions, and have almost made the apron an additional item of dress. Aprons were worn for every kind of work in town and country. They were made of all kinds of materials, from heavy sackcloth and flannels for rough work to cottons galore, and spotless white cotton or linen for dairy work, cooking or elsewhere in the home. When women servants went into uniforms in the nineteenth century aprons were a prominent item. Fancy aprons even appeared on social occasions, worn by hostesses at tea parties.

For heavy farm work in the eighteenth century and later, women would wear an apron over the usual bedgown, but on occasion in the heat they would appear in the fields wearing only a petticoat with visible stays and shift showing above the waist. The bedgown is shown frequently in eighteenth-century paintings of farm scenes, notably many of those by George Stubbs (1724–1806).

The bedgown, already mentioned as being unsuitably named, features frequently in eighteenth-century rural scenes – a loose, crossover one-piece garment, of flannel or wool, or, from the later eighteenth century, of cotton. It could be short or full-length and continued to be worn in the nineteenth century with little change. A detailed description of a countrywoman is given by George Eliot in *Adam Bede*. Though published in 1859, this book deals with the turn of the nineteenth century and is a

32 'The Enraged Musician: *a great scene by Hogarth. One of his own engravings, published by himself, 1741.*

country story, full of details about the country-side and the lives of simple, working people. Adam Bede's mother Lisbeth is described as

wearing 'a pure linen cap with a black band round it. The broad chest is covered with a buff neckerchief, and below this you see a short bed-gown made of blue-checkered linen, tied round the waist and descending to the hips, from whence there is a considerable length of linsey-wolsey petticoat'. The age of wool was passing,

33 *Hogarth's portrait of his servants, showing the under-the-chin caps then favoured by many women.*

but this was still the traditional dress of the working woman and as she awaits Adam 'she stands knitting rapidly and unconsciously with her work-hardened hands'. In another description, meticulous, like all those of the people in the novel, Lisbeth is 'a clean old woman, in a dark-striped linen gown, a red kerchief, and a linen cap'.

Other detailed descriptions of country dress are given in *Adam Bede*. They are particularly interesting because the book, as Adam points out, is set in a village that looks 'at the canals, an' th' aquaducts, an' th' coal-pit engines, and Arkwright's mills there at Cromford'. The dress is the dress of the people and the time. Adam is 'a stalwart workman in paper cap, leather breeches and dark-blue worsted stockings', which, incidentally, his mother is described as busily knitting as she awaits his return home at night. Hetty, a pretty girl, is dressed for butter-making and 'stands on little pattens', wears 'a pink and white handkerchief tucked into her low, plum-coloured stuff bodice' and has a linen butter-making apron with its bib, brown stockings and thick soled buckled shoes'. But on Sunday, dressed for church, she is 'in her Sunday hat and frock. For her hat was trimmed with pink, and her frock had pink roses sprinkled on a white ground'. It is evidently made of the newer cotton. For the squire's party she is again in pink and white. The squire is in bright blue frock-coat, the highest mode.

An older man, Mr Poyser, at church, 'was in his Sunday suit of drab, with a red and green watch-ribbon, having a large cornelian seal attached, pendant like a plumb-line from that promontory, where his watch-pocket was situated; a silk handkerchief of a yellow tone round his neck, and excellent gray-ribbed stockings, knitted by Mrs Poyser's own hand, setting off the proportions of his leg.' The little boys, nine and eleven, wear 'little fustian tailed coats and knee-breeches'.

How country dress could remain unchanged for long periods and, conversely, how change did at times come, is illustrated later by two passages in Hardy's novel, *Tess of the D'Urbervilles*. When Tess is reduced to tramping the country in search of work as a farm labourer, she is described as 'a figure which is part of the landscape; a fieldwoman pure and simple, in winter guise; a gray serge cape, a red woollen cravat, a stuff skirt covered by a whitey-brown rough wrapper, and buff-leather gloves.' This garb could belong to any period, any place.

Later on in the book, when Alec D'Urberville is trying desperately to break down her evasion of him and renew contact with her, he appears near her in her native village in a disguise which has become outdated: 'The grotesqueness of his appearance in a gathered smockfrock, such as was now worn only by the most old-fashioned of

the labourers, ... chilled her as to its bearing.' He explains: 'The smockfrock, which I saw hanging for sale as I came along, was an afterthought, that I mightn't be noticed.'

The London Shops

The busy, bustling London shopping scene, English dress and the London crowds of the later eighteenth century fascinated a much-travelled German woman visitor who spent a few crowded weeks there in 1786. She was Sophie von la Roche, author and educationalist, who kept a detailed diary for her family at home. She explained indefatigably and missed nothing.

Once landed at Harwich Sophie started recording her observations. At first sight she is critical of Englishwomen: 'Nor do I care for the Englishwomen here as yet, caps, hats and clothes look as though an eternal wind-storm raged along this coast, allowing no single garment to remain in place.'

Transport to London was excellent and Colchester enchanted her: 'As we drove past, enjoyed the fine shops jut out at both sides of the front doors like big, broad oriels, having fine large window-panes, behind which wares were displayed, so that these shops look far more elegant than those in Paris.'

London exceeded all her expectations: 'It is almost impossible to express how well everything is organized in London. Every article is made more attractive to the eye than in Paris or in any other town.' Dress fabrics attract her attention in the shops: 'We especially noticed a cunning device for showing women's materials. Whether they are silks, chintzes or muslins, they hang down in folds behind the fine high windows so that the effect of that material, as it would be in the ordinary folds of a woman's dress, can be studied.'

She is surprised that English women wear hats on all occasions, and when settled in lodgings her first need is that a friend's 'eldest daughter is getting me a cap and hat, as women here may not go out without a hat ... I am very glad that women of my age wear caps under

34 *Ackermann's* Repository *in 1809 records
how luxury has come to London's shops.*

their hats, and that I shall not have much
trouble or expense with my coiffure'.

At the inn where she stays in London 'within
the hour my eyes had grown fully acquainted
with the costume worn by the maids, women of
middle-class and the children. The former
almost all wear black tammy [a coarse twilled
worsted] petticoats, rather stiff and heavily
stitched and over these long English calico or
linen frocks . . . here they are sensibly fashioned
to the figure. Further, they mostly wear white
aprons, though the servants and working-
women often appear in striped linen gowns. The
caps really resemble those seen on English
engravings, and simple black taffeta hats
besides with black ribbons fitting right down on
to the head.'

52

Caught in rain after a theatre and unable to find a conveyance she laments that 'my black hat with the embroidered crape was ruined, and I had to get a new one'. Hats continue to be a topic. Visiting a friend, Madame La Fite, at Windsor, where she met Fanny Burney at a ladies' literary tea party and the guests were busy with 'fancy work sewing bands of fine muslin', she continues: 'Next day Madam La Fite gave me one of her hats to wear, and I

35 *An eighteenth-century milliner's shop: a cartoon.*

accompanied her to church at Windsor Castle.'

But Oxford Street and its crowds remain her great love: 'We strolled up and down lovely Oxford Street this evening, for some goods look more attractive by artificial light. Just imagine, dear children, a street taking half an hour to cover from end to end, with double rows of

53

brightly shining lamps ... and the pavement, inlaid with flag-stones, can stand six people deep and allows one to gaze at the splendidly lit shops in comfort ... Up to eleven o'clock at night there are as many people along this street as at Frankfurt during the fair.'

Finally, before leaving London, 'this afternoon I took a walk up and down that lovely Oxford Street, so as to take a good look at all the houses and the numerous shops ... I found another shop here like the one in Paris, containing every possible make of woman's shoe ... But the linen-shops are the loveliest; every kind of white wear, ... and any species of linen, can be had. Nightcaps for ladies and children, trimmed with muslin or various kinds of Brussels lace, more exquisitely stitched than any I ever saw before.'

She visits Warren Hastings and his German wife at Windsor and during the visit 'Mrs Hastings tied a shawl round me before going out in the garden and I thought it a delightful trick of fortune to have placed me beside the Governor of East India, ... wrapped in an East Indian material more costly than silk, much lighter and also much warmer than the latter'.

A very different view of London shops had been given a few years earlier by another writer, though this time not from far. Nor was she any stranger to London. She was Fanny Burney and, looking at the shopping scene from the other side of the counter, she does not find much improvement on the old days to keep pace with the greater availability of goods which delighted Sophie. In some respects the old pattern of the shop on the ground floor and the family living above seems to have persisted.

Fanny Burney in her first publication *Evelina* (1778) depicts such arrangements as very unsatisfactory when Evelina is taken to London by her disagreeable grandmother Madame Duval to see and be under the wing of a relation, Mr Branghton, a silversmith, and his family at his shop at Snow Hill. 'The Branghtons' house is small and inconvenient,' she writes, 'though the shop, which takes in all the ground floor, is large and commodious.... We were conducted up

two pair of stairs, for the dining-room, Mr Branghton told us, was *let*.'

Taken to her lodgings in Holborn Evelina finds: 'Our rooms are large and not inconvenient; our landlord is a hosier ... my present position is, in every respect, very unenviable.' She continues: 'Yesterday morning, we received an invitation to dine and spend the day at Mr Branghton's.' His two daughters are not dressed when the visitors arrive, so Evelina is taken up the two flights of stairs to see them. The sisters are reproved by their father: 'Here's your aunt and cousin, and M. Du Bois, all waiting, and ne'er a room to take them in.' Miss Polly says: 'Can't they stay in the shop till we're dressed?' So stools were procured in the shop. They stay there till dinner is ready, 'when we again mounted up two pair of stairs', for a terrible dinner, with things being fetched from downstairs. After dinner Polly says: 'Don't you think, Miss, it's very dull sitting upstairs here? We'd better go down to *shop*, and then we shall see the people go by.' There are arguments, then the elder sister declares: 'I'll sure you, Cousin, we have some very genteel people pass by our shop sometimes: Polly and I always go and sit there, when we've cleaned ourselves.' 'Yes, Miss,' cries the brother, 'they do nothing else all day long, when father don't scold them.' So – it was at length decided that they should go to the shop.

If it is permissible to move on a few years and have another look at shops, probably a more balanced view is that given by Jane Austen, who several times mentions shopping as a pleasant occupation, and one enjoyed by her kind of ordinary people, admittedly a slightly privileged country group living near attractive towns of not too large a size.

Though London and Bath had special attractions, Jane refers to local drapers' shops more in her letters to her sister Cassandra than in the novels, but Emma, in the novel of that name (1816) goes shopping twice at Ford's, in Highbury, near her home at Hartfield, not far from London. The main visit described is the one made by Emma with Frank Churchill, a

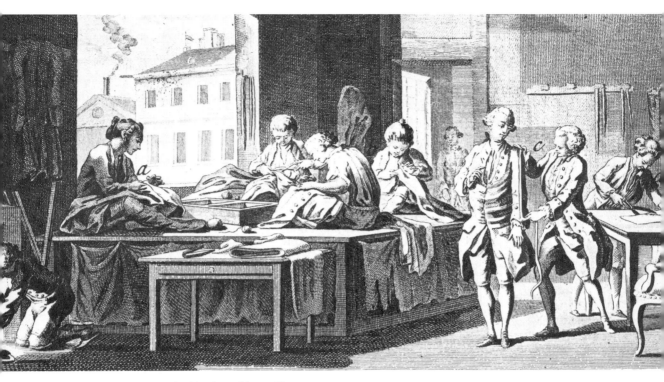

36 *A men's tailor at work in his shop, his staff sitting cross-legged beside him as he measures a customer. From Diderot's* Encyclopédie.

favourite visitor, who, as they approach Ford's, exclaims: 'Ha! this must be the very shop that everybody attends every day of their lives, as my father informs me. He comes to Highbury himself, he says, six days out of the seven, and has always business at Ford's. If it be not inconvenient to you, pray let us go in, that I may prove myself to belong to the place; to be a true citizen of Highbury I must buy something at Ford's ... I daresay they sell gloves.' To which Emma replies: 'Oh! yes, gloves and everything,' and in they go to make the purchase from 'the sleek, well-tied parcels of "Men's Beavers" and "York Tan"' brought down for their inspection, these being favoured styles of leather glove at the time.

37 *The Tailor – from* The Book of English Trades, *1803*.

55

5
Beginnings of the Industrial Revolution

New Inventions and the Cotton Industry

Just when the industrial revolution began is almost infinitely arguable, but in the present context two points are essential to the story and are beyond any doubt. Britain was the world leader in this new movement that was to transform the world and in Britain cotton fabrics were the first major product to be made by the new processes. Cotton was to transform ordinary women's dress.

The quickening of science and invention had by the middle of the eighteenth century reached a point at which increased national production and manufacture of goods, for both home and overseas trade, with the aim of increasing wealth for the nation and its people, was the dominant purpose. For growth it was natural to look first at the main established activities and of these textile production remained first and foremost, as well as the oldest. The greatest obstacle to growth there was a shortage of spun yarns. Ways of speeding up the spinning and weaving of cloth were needed and of these spinning was the more urgent, because weavers were more and more being held up by lack of yarn prepared for them by the hand-spinners – the only kind of spinners then known. It took ten of them to keep one weaver fully supplied with his needs.

It was therefore in that direction that inven-

38 *Spinning in 1808: moving towards mechanization.*

tiveness was mainly directed. The first success-ful 'spinning machine' was the 'jenny' (a collo-quialism from 'engine') of James Hargreaves, a poor weaver in the cotton trade in Blackburn. In 1764 he invented the 'jenny', devised to spin eight threads at once. It had eight vertical spindles operating on the great wheel principle, with eight driving bands controlling eight threads. In 1766 it was improved to take 16, and it was patented in 1770. It was violently at-tacked by angry hand-spinners who, fearing the loss of their livelihood, destroyed some of the machines. Hargreaves was forced out and was driven to Nottingham, where he adapted his invention to provide cotton yarn for the hosiery trade. But 20,000 'jennies' were in use, mainly in Lancashire, by the turn of the century. It had the great advantage that it could be used in any cottage, and eventually could work 80 spindles. Hargreaves, however, drew no benefit from it and died a poor man.

The weakness of the 'jenny' was that its threads were not strong enough for warping. This problem was solved by Sir Richard Arkwright's water frame or roller-spinning ma-chine of 1768. It was so heavy that it could not be controlled manually but had to be powered, originally by horse power and then by a water wheel, so it was limited to factory use. Unlike Hargreaves, however, Arkwright prospered after some set-backs, got his first factory in 1771 at Cromford, in Derbyshire, was knighted and died in 1792 with a fortune of half-a-million pounds. He had lived to see the first steam engine supplying power for his invention, which had multiplied output and provided the finer yet stronger thread as required. He had started life as a barber travelling round Lancashire buying the long hair of country girls to make into wigs. Carlyle said of him: 'What a historical phenomenon is that bag-cheeked, pot-bellied, much-enduring much-inventing barber.'

Third of the early textile pioneer inventors was Samuel Crompton, a Bolton weaver, who in 1779 produced a machine called the spinning mule because it was a cross between the inven-tions of his two predecessors, producing finer and stronger thread and also capable of being used at home as well as in a factory. In fact it was for many years used only in cottages. It was difficult to make and factory production of machines proceeded slowly because of the scar-city of that new breed, the good mechanic. The machine brought prosperity to Crompton's home town, but he died in poverty in 1827.

Various other inventions from this time failed to make an immediate impact, among them a power loom invented in 1785 by a clergyman, Dr Edmund Cartwright. It was large and clumsy, difficult to make and operate, and when 400 were installed in a Manchester factory in 1792 the building was burnt down by angry workers. Hand-weavers as a result of this hos-tility to machines had a bonanza for a time, workers earning large wages, especially for making fine woollens. The power loom did not come into substantial use until after 1850.

The development of weaving was mainly dependent on the improvement in spinning machinery, to speed up yarn supplies, so chiefly for that reason there was no immediate suc-cessor to one of the first inventions of all in textiles, the 'flying shuttle' of John Kay, of 1733. Its purpose was to speed up weaving by carrying the weft threads automatically across the warp by means of hammers on a string or wire which the weaver could operate with one hand. Cloth could thereby be wider than the limits of the weaver's arm-stretch. It again caused fury among hand-weavers who saw it as a threat to their livelihood and Kay died in poverty.

The new developments were much more easily adaptable to cotton than to wool, the fibres of which were difficult to handle mechan-ically. Certain processes in the preparation of wool were also a source of problems for spinning machines at first. These were eventually overcome, and in 1787 there was one long-fibred worsted wool already being machine-spun in a Yorkshire mill. Linen was even slower to re-spond to the new system. Neither could com-pete with cotton in price, so on all counts cotton was the immediate winner.

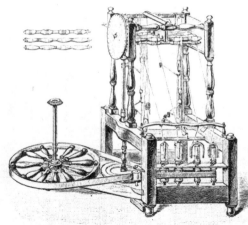

39 *Mechanization speeds up cloth production. Left, Arkwright's Water Frame (1769); below, Hargreaves' Spinning Jenny (1756); bottom, Crompton's Mule (1755).*

40 *Above; interior of mule-spinning factory, 1835.*   41 *Below; power-loom weaving, 1835.*

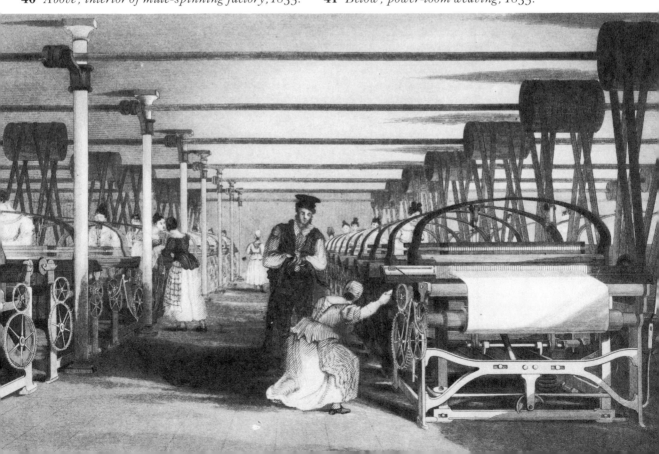

42 *Factory scene, 1839, with women and children, and managers in the background.*

The general effect of the machines was therefore greatly to increase the output of cotton materials, to improve their range immensely, especially in the production of fine muslins, and also, for the first time in history, to make dress fabrics cheap. This was a revolution for ordinary people. Hitherto all materials had been expensive. Now there were fabrics that were available in great variety, often beautifully coloured or attractively patterned, costing the public a fraction of what had previously been paid.

A Dress Revolution for Ordinary People

These cottons made history in several ways. Cottons were cheap, attractive and production of them was capable of almost limitless expansion to meet the need. They were unlike wool or linen materials, which were limited by the size of flocks of sheep and of areas of Britain suited to growing flax. But because of this there grew up not only success and new possibilities for ordinary dress but also one of the blots on the clothing industry – of which many were to follow. This was the nefarious 'three-way' or Triangular trade, by which British merchants, mainly from Bristol but later also from Liverpool, sailed to Africa with manufactured goods. These they exchanged there for negroes, to be taken by them as slave-labour to the West Indies and the American colonies of North America. There the human cargo was exchanged for supplies of cotton, brought home to Britain to be manufactured into much-needed dress and household textiles. This was done in factories where working conditions were often so appalling that they constituted something like another kind of slave labour, a parallel not generally seen at the time.

44 *Innovations in dress materials. The calico-printer, as shown in* The Book of English Trades, *1823.*

43 *Carding, drawing and roving in a cotton factory in the 1840s.*

45 *Cotton comes to the fore: elegance in a summer dinner dress in printed cotton, with lace frill at hem, 1823–25.*

In the home market the opportunity of buying cheap, attractive fabrics for making up into clothes was little less than a miracle for ordinary people. Records such as Parson Woodforde's Diary (1758–1802) will show what full advantage was quickly taken of this. In a very short time cotton dresses were the general wear of women of all classes; for the first time

fashionable and popular taste coincided. The French Revolution, the 'back to nature' cult of Rousseau, and the vogue for 'Grecian' modes all gave immense scope to every kind of cotton, from plain or printed fabrics of modest price and simple style to delicate muslins, embroidered or lace-trimmed, sought after by the fashionable woman.

There was another more practical and even more important result of the cotton revolution, though it was probably not the aim of the inventors. Cotton, unlike woollens, silks, brocades and other previously fashionable fabrics, could be easily and successfully washed. England, for the first time, took an immense pride in cleanliness and freshly laundered, light-coloured cottons became much sought after and admired.

More important than the visible freshness of clothes was the effect on health. English people came to be observed by visiting foreigners for their cleanliness; a visitor from France commented: 'English women and men are very clean: not a day passes by without their washing their hands, arms, faces, necks and throats in cold water, and that in winter as well as summer.' The effect of clean clothes on health was important. Dorothy George says in her *England in Transition*: 'The new washable cottons, which were universally worn by women, replaced such things as linsey-woolsey petticoats padded with horsehair or cotton-wool, and leather stays, worn till they dropped to pieces from dirt.'

Although men did not wear cotton to the same extent as women, the years 1794–1816 were the heyday of Beau Brummell, whose leadership in men's fashions was based on a passion for an immaculate cleanliness in simple, beautifully cut clothes – for spotless linen, shining white cravats and personal hygiene.

Coincidentally medicine, and especially popular medicine, was improving. Five new hospitals were founded during the first half of the century. Midwifery was being improved extensively. Dispensaries were being set up where the poor could go for medicines and

46 *Purple silk pelisse and flower-printed cotton dress of about 1828.*

by the introduction of synthetic fibres in the twentieth century. Cotton is one of the oldest of yarns, and had been grown in about 60 countries for centuries, mainly in Egypt, India, China, parts of America and Russia, but it needed a warm climate and could not be grown in Western Europe.

It can be traced back to 3000 BC in Indian tombs and it was from that country that painted cottons were imported into Europe from the seventeenth century and, being attractive, novel, scarce and costly, had a certain prestigious vogue among the wealthy and fashionable in England, especially in very fine muslins imported from India and coveted by elegant ladies.

England's first importer of cotton yarns was the East India Company, founded in 1612, which also brought in 'calicoe' from Calcutta and fine muslins from Mosul, all costly fabrics in short supply. Defoe early in the eighteenth century mentioned a vogue for these, especially in printed fabrics. When the East India Company's monopoly of trade with India ended in 1813 the West Indies began to supply a lot of raw cotton, but the growth of Britain's use of cotton yarn had developed considerably by then – supplies had been brought back from the southern plantations of North America by explorers. As their discoveries extended they found further supplies in Mexico and Peru. By 1800 the cotton industry had overtaken the woollen one in Britain.

So rapid had been the growth of cotton imports that in 1791 Britain transported 38,000 negroes from Africa to the cotton plantations of America, which was more than half the total European slave trade for that year.

Though machine-woven and machine-spun cloths came into existence in the latter part of the eighteenth century, the craft of hand-weaving declined only slowly, and indeed lingered on, both in its humbler guises and in the prestige production of luxury woollens, some of which persist to this day. A picture of an aspect of the craft which looked back was recorded in George Eliot's story of a hand weaver, *Silas*

advice. Paving and lighting for streets, water supplies, draining and the demolition of slums were being put in hand, not only in London but also in other main towns, where growth of trade and industry was drawing in workers from rural areas.

Cotton, of course, was by no means new, even in England, when it created the eighteenth-century revolution in everyday dressing – a revolution as great in many ways as that caused

47 *Printed dresses in cotton of 1830–40 by Harrods, with billowing skirts and full sleeves.*

48 *Purple and beige striped cotton dress, about 1843–45.*

49 *Simpler dress for men in 1791: a natural look, almost country-like; coat turned back forming tails and casually half-buttoned; easy neckline, ribbed stockings and plain shoes.*

50 *Undress – that is, informal dressing, for 1799, in simple cotton dresses, one with contrasting dark tippet.*

Marner, published in 1861, but set in the early years of the nineteenth century, in the last lingering of 'the days when the spinning-wheels hummed busily in the farmhouses and even great ladies, clothed in silk and thread-lace, had their toy spinning wheels of polished oak'.

Some of the last hand-weavers were linen-weavers, often, like Silas Marner, voluntary exiles from towns, so that there were 'in districts far away among the lanes, or deep in the bosom of the hills, certain pallid undersized men, who, by the side of the brawny country-folk, looked like the remains of a disinherited race'. They were linen-weavers, emigrants from towns, regarded as aliens. With a 'bent tread-mill attitude, at work, Silas Marner would go across the fields 'to fetch and carry home his work'.

It paid better to be self-employed in the country than to work for a dealer in a town. Silas earned his five guineas a week, 'five bright guineas put into his hand', but he 'saw no vision

51 *A country scene:* The Splenetic Traveller *by Thomas Bewick (1758–1828).*

beyond countless days of weaving ... the live-long day he sat at his loom, his ear filled with its monotony, his eyes bent down on the slow growth of sameness in the brownish web'. A humble man, collecting and delivering as well as weaving, he was the old-time weaver, working for humble people.

Shopping for a Country Parsonage

An almost day-to-day diary kept from 1758 to 1802 with no thought of posterity, completely unknown until 1924 and with its five volumes appearing between then and 1931, is a rich trove of information about the dress and habits of ordinary people of its time in a secluded but typical Norfolk village. Parson Woodforde's *Diary of a Country Parson* records his life at Weston Longeville and all the people who shared it – his niece Nancy who kept house for him, his two maid servants, his man and boy – all living comfortably on his income of £400 a year. It also includes visits to Bath and London, and shopping wherever he goes.

Why, after nearly 200 years, is it so very well worth while following Parson Woodforde on his clothes-buying expeditions? For one thing, because, more than anyone except Pepys, he has a rare faculty of taking the reader with him wherever he goes. On his shopping trips everything is as real and immediate as if it were happening to us today. So is the day-to-day life of his household. But more practically, most of his purchases of fabrics and his general dress details are dated in the 1790s and give a first-hand account of how fully the new inexpensive cottons had captured the everyday market of master, mistress and servants, even in the remote country. All the details are there in his words.

It is immediately evident that daily life in the country has moved fast since the diaries of the seventeenth century. Immense strides have been made in travel and communications. Norwich, only a few miles from the parsonage, is an impressive shopping centre, where nearly everything can be bought with ease and comfort, and it is regularly visited.

On one occasion Parson Woodforde records that 'Nancy bought a new black beaver hat with purple Cockade and band. She gave for it 1.3.0. She bought it of one Caley in the Market Place. I also bought a new hat of him, pd him for it 1.1.0. Whilst my niece was at Barths, Stay and Habit Maker, I walked to Bacons and paid him for Knox's Sermons ... To 11 Dozen of Buttons Coat and Waistcoat, some Italian, some Clay's Paper ones, all black at Bakers ... Called at my Mercers, Smiths, and bespoke a Coat, Waistcoat and Breeches of him. Then went to my Taylors Forsetter, and told him to make a Suit of Livery for Briton' (his man). No shopping problems here.

Again at Norwich: 'I walked out with Nancy to Miss Brownes to see the Fashions. Gave Nancy a very handsome Sash &c. paid for the same, 0.18.0 ... I walked about by myself & pd

52 *The countryman of the early nineteenth century. The drover, in white coat, yellow waistcoat, red and white spotted handkerchief, blue and white striped stockings, and badge on left arm.*

53 *A postman of 1813, wearing a red coat with blue facings and a yellow waistcoat.*

more Bills. To Smith, Mercer, pd 8.4.0. To Frank, Barber, for a Wigg, pd 1.1.0. To Mrs Brewster, Haberdasher, pd 3.10.6. ... Nancy bought her a pretty Hat suitable to the Sash.'

Next day at Norwich: 'At Graham's Shop for a pr of black Silk Stockings and changing another pair that I bought there last Year which did not fit me, pd 0.16.0. To four pair of white worsted Gauze Do. pd 0.7.4.'

A considerable number of purchases are made still from men who call at the house with their offerings. Thus: 'To a Man who comes from Windham and carries about stuffs for Gowns &c, for 27 yards and half at 9d per yard 1.0.6. Gave both my Maids a Gown apiece of it and of the same Colour, something of the Pea Green. Gave Nancy also, to make a Skirt for her of a light blue six yds.'

A regular caller is 'one Aldridge who called here this Morning with a Cart with things, for $\frac{1}{2}$ yard of canbrick pd 0.5.0. Of ditto for corded Muslin $\frac{1}{2}$ Yard for the Maids 0.3.6. and which I gave between them for Caps'. There is a bigger order for Aldridge on another occasion.

Purchases from Aldridge recur and show that cotton has taken over: 'To 7 Yards of Cotton a mixed Colour of black, purple and Green, for a morning Gown for myself, this Morning of Aldridge at 2s/2d per Yrd. pd 0.15.2. Of Ditto for 7 Yrds of white Cotton for a lining to the above at 1s/0d per Yrd pd 0.7.0.'

Again: 'To 4 Yards and 3 Quarters of Cambrick for Handkerchiefs for myself, at 6 Shillings a Yard, paid Aldridge 1.8.6. which will make me five good Handkerchiefs. And a small one for Nancy besides.'

Finally, a big order for inexpensive cottons from Aldridge. 'Aldridge who goes abt. with Cottons &c called here ... To Aldridge for 14 Yards of Cotton, at 2s/3d. pd 1.11.6 which I gave to my two Maids, a Gown each. To Aldridge also, for 8 Yrds. of Cotton at 2/6, 1.0.0. which I gave to Miss Woodforde. Also for 7 Yards of Cotton for a Gown for myself, at 2s/2d. pd 0.15.0. Pd him likewise for a Marcella-Waistcoat Piece Yellow Ground $\frac{3}{4}$ yrd square, for Ben 0.8.0. To Aldridge also, for 2 Silk

54 *The pedlar played a large part in life at the Rectory.*

Handkerchiefs from Spital Fields, Chocolate Ground & Yellow Spots, pd 11.0. One of which I gave to Ben and the other to Boy, Tim. Paid Aldridge in the whole 4.5.2.'

Long summer visits to his own county of Somerset are undertaken every two or three summers by Parson Woodforde and Nancy, and a stop is usually made at Bath, which provides new scope for shopping for clothes and other personal requirements.

At Bath 'I walked about Bath with my Sister Pounsett & Daughter and Nancy a shopping. At Percival's Shop in Milsom Street for three Pieces of Muslin ten Yards each Piece and one Yard & half wide – very great bargain, I paid 3.15.0 which was only twenty five Shillings apiece. I gave one Piece to my sister Pounsett, another to my Niece Pounsett and the other Nancy had.'

A few days in London could also usually be encompassed in these cross-country journeys, now possible because of the great improvements being made in the speed and efficiency and

55 *Country life at the beginning of the nineteenth century. A gardener, from a print of 1804.*

56 *Fishing for whiting at Margate, 1834. Note the top hat, now very widely worn.*

comfort of coaches. London was still the country's leading shopping centre, a great attraction with opportunities not possible elsewhere.

On one London visit: 'After breakfast we took a Coach and went to Charlesworth, Haberdasher in Great Russel Street, Covent Garden and there Nancy bought divers things – I lent her the same 1.1.0. From thence we walked to Southampton Street very near the last Place, and there at a very good Linen-Drapers Shop kept by a Mr Jeremy, a very civil Man, bought some Table Linnen, ... a piece of Holland, Cravats &c. paid there 13.6.0.'

In London he also 'walked to a Milleners Shop and I bought 3 dressed Caps for Nancy, for my Sister Pounsett and her little girl, with about 10 Yards of Ribband besides pd there 1.11.6.'

After another visit, he 'gave my two Maids a Cotton Gown apiece that I bought for them in London cost me 1.8.0. Gave my Servant Man Ben a Waistcoat Piece 0.6.0. Gave my Servant Lad John, in Cash 0.2.6.'

He went 'to Reeves Hosiery Warehouse in the Strand early this Morning for a pair of Boot Stockings, pd 0.4.6. For brown travelling Cap pd 0.4.0. for a cotton and worsted shaving Cap, pd 0.2.3. For a Silk Purse at the same Shop, pd 0.2.0.' Finally, 'Soon after Breakfast I walked with Nancy to her Mantua Maker Miss Ryder, Southampton Buildings, Chancery Lane.'

The terms on which the Maids are engaged do not seem to have included clothes, but gifts of cotton for dresses are frequently made to them, of the same material in each case, though uniform was not at the time worn by women servants. In the case of a boy, newly engaged, the arrangement about clothes was different: 'I am to give him per Annum for Wages. 1.1.0. A Coat and Waist coat and Hat when wanted, to allow him something for being washed out and mended – and his Friends to find him in Stockings and Shoes &.'

Nancy does some sewing, but not by any means all. She is described as occupying herself 'netting her Apron' while her uncle read a History of England to her. On another occasion he gives her 'some Muslin to make a shawl. Nancy completely finished this new spotted Apron – and very pretty it looks'.

When Nancy is in Somerset, on one occasion she 'had a brown Silk gown trimmed with Burr brought home this Evening by Cary from her Mantua maker, Miss Bell. It was a very good rich silk that I gave her which formerly belonged to my poor Aunt Parr, whose effects came to me'. Handing on clothes was a usual procedure. A visiting cousin is given 'a Pr of Shoes, a Pr of Stockings, a Pr of Breeches and Shirt and Stock, and an old Coat and Waistcoat'. Nancy does an occasional repair for her uncle: 'Gave Nancy this Morning for well Mending a Pair of Velveret Breeches for me 1s 0.'

Even washing-day problems engage Parson Woodforde's attention. He tells how his maid,

Betty, 'went to Norwich to buy my two old washer-women Mary Heavers and Nan Gooch a new Gown apiece which I intend giving them'.

On another occasion he again thinks of the washer-women. There is an entry in the diary for '2 Coloured Handkerchiefs for my two washer-women, Dawning & Richmond.'

The New Simplicity

From about 1790 a sudden simplicity revolutionized women's dress and greatly modified men's, lasting with few basic changes for nearly 30 years. It affected ordinary people as well as the fashionable. It is generally attributed to changing social, political and artistic changes, but it is still even more difficult wholly to explain than are most of fashion's variations.

It was not in fact quite so drastic as would seem at first sight. In the case of women the immense panniers featured so lavishly in surviving fashionable clothes and recorded in costume histories were a minority fashion, like the earlier farthingale wearable only by the few and for special occasions. General wear for women of all classes during the eighteenth century was usually, as previously, a fitted or loose bodice and a full skirt, the latter sometimes open-fronted, showing a decorative petticoat, which had not yet become an undergarment. Such a dress was within the means of the middle-class woman and suitable to her needs. It could be enhanced or simplified to suit everybody. The mantua, already described, was worn on many occasions, also by all classes. It was still usually a one-piece gown, simpler, looser and more casual. The even more loose-fitting bedgown, so unsuitably named, continued to be working gear well into the nineteenth century.

But now ordinary and fashionable women took to dresses of almost child-like simplicity – in fact they had started as the wear of little girls in the 1770s. Petticoats were minimal, corsets sometimes abandoned. Full advantage was taken of the recently available inexpensive cottons and muslins, eminently suited to such dresses; these fabrics undoubtedly helped to make the new fashion widespread, but it cannot

57 *Simplicity in women's dress spread to all classes from the end of the eighteenth century, and only gradually disappeared. Here, are, Regency Belles of 1803–5, both in slim, high-waisted dresses. On the right, cream silk on twill ground, by-passing every curve. On the left, a shawl is added, and an outsize poke-bonnet conceals the face too.*

71

be seen solely as an offshoot of the large-scale manufacture of cotton.

In general the formality of the Augustan age was outgrown and a reaction to informality was natural. It was seen in poetry, in a love of Nature, in the doctrines of Rousseau, but these influences were mainly for the educated classes. In a wider sense the French Revolution (1789) was a great social leveller, and its mood affected England, though more slowly than France. There the full impact of the new fashions was quickly felt. Fanny Burney, middle class and no follower or respecter of fashion, went to Paris in 1801 after the Peace of Amiens, and, as a biographer records: 'First came the business, always faintly amusing to Fanny, of revising a rustic wardrobe to suit Parisian fashion. She speaks of "the exclamations which followed the examination of my attire. This won't do! That you can never wear! . . . Three petticoats, no one wears more than one! Stays? Everyone has left off even corsets! Shift sleeves? Not a soul now

58 *The old-style formal dress for men was caricatured by Rowlandson in* Men of Fashion *(c. 1790).*

59 *Morning and evening ladies' dresses for 1807, the latter with a shawl; the fashionable gentleman is wearing evening dress with an outsize cravat: as shown in the magazine* Le Beau Monde.

60 *Back to nature: Sir Walter Scott's daughters in peasant dress, by Sir David Wilkie, 1817.*

61 *A model, in the Victoria & Albert Museum, of a well-dressed businessman of the early nineteenth century. Thomas Coutts, founder of the bank bearing his name, wears a black cloth coat, waistcoat and breeches, with a beaver hat. Coutts died in 1822.*

wears even a chemise!'' Fanny solved the problem characteristically by wearing what she had always worn, regardless of the mode.'

The dress of men also became simpler from about 1790, for the same reasons – a changing social climate and a more relaxed view of life. In general men's fashion was less formal, more natural, and this was mainly seen in a liking for country clothes, often based on what was worn by ordinary men and lower-class dress. This reversal of the usual rule, of fashion coming from the top, was very evident in the wearing of the riding coat and easy breeches, more casual neckwear and a general modification of existing fashionable dress.

There were, by the end of the eighteenth century, two main versions of the man's coat, both of which set the stamp on future male dress of the ordinary middle classes and which were increasingly copied by the upper classes, instead of vice-versa. This was partly because men of fashion were now conforming to the new pattern of a busy city life instead of permanent leisure in country pursuits. Based on the earlier long coat, both new coats at first had the fronts turned back to form tails. The more formal version was close-fitting and from it evolved both the tailed morning coat and the evening coat, both still worn at times.

The other new arrival was the man's 'frock' coat, based on an artisan's coat and giving away its origins by being at first called, like the latter, the 'frock'. With a collar but no lapels, it was worn widely from the mid-eighteenth century for all but formal occasions. One variation became a riding coat. Later, as Phillis Cunnington says, the frock coat became 'the hall-mark of the 19th century' much worn by the middle class in a new guise, waisted, single-breasted, with a roll or stand-up collar, buttons to the waist. From 1825 it had lapels. By 1840 there was a shorter variation, worn for sporting occasions.

Trousers first began to replace breeches about 1803, and were becoming general by about 1807, to the surprise of most people. Breeches after that were mainly worn for sporting occasions, principally riding, but also, in a formal

62 *The evolution of men's dress: a satirist's view of 1820 in* Bond Street Loungers *by R. Dighton, who surveys two dukes, two earls and a notability of the time in the variations presented by contemporary modes – but always with top hats.*

style, for some evening wear of a ceremonial kind, such as Court dress and the traditional dress of judges, high churchmen and others.

The frock coat remained the usual wear for men throughout the nineteenth century in business, trade, the professions and, in general, for all above the working class level in the new, ever-growing industrial world. The top hat was also normally worn. Not till the end of the nineteenth century did the lounge jacket, an up-market version of the almost timeless jacket or jerkin (a rougher jacket, often of leather) of the working man, become round-the-clock wear for men in general, as part of the 'bespoke' town suit and as the blazer, sports jacket, 'smoking jacket', and after World War II as a dinner jacket practically ousting the evening 'tail suit' or 'tails' for all but very formal events. Most of these varieties of jacket could be single- or double-breasted, according to choice or minor fashion changes from time to time.

Meantime, like men, women did not leave their new-found fashions unchanged. Cotton in the English climate was not always warm enough for general wear, but various solutions for this were devised. Parson Woodforde describes a visit from Mrs Custance: 'Though June, it was very cold indeed again today, so cold that Mrs Custance came walking in her Spencer with a Bosom-Friend.'

The spencer, originally a short coat worn by men from the start of the nineteenth century, took its name from Earl Spencer (1758–1834) and a version was adopted by women. It has been worn ever since. At first it was waist-length, long-sleeved, with revers and collar, and in this form was worn from the 1790s till about 1825, with the slim dresses. Then it became more casual, sometimes knitted, sometimes sleeveless, and at times worn under the dress, from the later nineteenth century into the twentieth. Though the name is now rarely used, something similar is still often worn among today's variety of 'layered' garments. Probably the spencer could be regarded as the prototype of the ubiquitous cardigan, worn by both men and women.

The Bosom Friend was a kind of tippet to protect the bare throat and chest, and its mention here in 1799 antedates the reference in the New Oxford Dictionary by two years. The reference to the spencer does the same by four years.

Another Woodforde diary date of interest here is that of a visit to Norwich in 1790 on which Nancy and her uncle see 'Lord Orford's droll-dressed Militia Men in Norwich, red Cloth Slops and loose white Trousers'. Men's trousers, whose origins are ascribed to peasant, sailors' and army wear, were thus in evidence before they were adopted by civilians early in the next century, with, it is said, the encouragement of George IV.

The Shawl

When in 1786 Sophie von la Roche expressed her delight at being presented with an East Indian shawl 'more costly than silk, much lighter and also much warmer than the latter' by the Governor of East India on her visit to him and his wife at Windsor, she was appropriately grateful for what was then a rare and coveted acquisition anywhere in Western Europe.

At that time such shawls, though they would be copied in Britain later and have a long-lasting vogue among all classes of women, with many variations of style and price, had to be imported from the East, were laboriously hand-woven of the finest cashmere in traditional designs, and therefore were very costly and highly prized. The genuine ones remained so. In Mrs Gaskell's *North and South*, published in 1855, their prestige remains strong among the prosperous middle-class people depicted. A bride's mother says: 'I have spared no expense in her trousseau. She has all the beautiful Indian shawls and scarfs the General gave to me, but which I shall never wear again.' 'She is a lucky girl,' replies another mother ... 'Helen had set her heart upon an Indian shawl, but really when I found what an extravagant price was asked, I was obliged, to refuse her ... What kinds are they? Delhi? with the lovely little borders?'

The bride's cousin, Margaret, has to show the shawls. 'So Margaret went down laden with shawls, and snuffing up their spicy Eastern smell... Her aunt asked her to stand as a sort of lay figure on which to display them ... Margaret's tall, finely made figure... set off the long beautiful folds of the gorgeous shawls ... She touched the shawls gently as they hung around her and took a pleasure in their soft feel and their brilliant colours.'

Edith later comments: 'But really Indian shawls are very perfect things of their kind.' A masculine comment is: 'Their prices are very perfect, too. Nothing wanting.'

Although it is recorded thus at a middle-class level, the shawl was probably the most classless, widely worn and generally approved item of wear among women from the late eighteenth century for nearly a hundred years. Since then it has continued to be worn, in some form, for some purpose, without a break, by innumerable kinds of women.

The shawl was the perfect accompaniment of the new light, simple cotton and muslin dresses worn by all classes of women during the last part of the eighteenth century. Often with short sleeves and low-cut necks, and with a diminished underpinning of corset and petticoats, these dresses called for an extra layer for warmth on most occasions. A shawl was ideal, wearable in many ways, easily picked up or discarded, with no problems of size or fit. That the eastern, costly imported versions should be copied was obvious. This was particularly tempting because the shawl was technically the ideal cross between the old hand-weaving and the new machine processes being developed in Britain, many of which were bringing new skills to the manufacture of fine, gossamer-like fabrics.

Production of cashmere shawls with patterns copied from the Indian ones began at Norwich, notable for its fine woollens, at the end of the eighteenth century. Then it started up in Edinburgh. But very soon it moved to the town which was to become world-famous for its shawls and to give its own name to the types it

63 *Paisley shawl of the early nineteenth century, when the vogue was at its height.*

established in popular favour from then to today. From the early nineteenth century the 'Paisley shawl' has been the universal name for the item, 'Paisley pattern' the universal name for the types of design based on the original versions imported from the East.

There were good reasons for this. Paisley had a long tradition of skill in weaving and, being in a damp, flax-growing area, was used to making fine linens. The shawls were usually made of fine wool and silk, or of wool or silk, and, from about 1845, of cotton. Patterns were traditionally woven into them, but cotton ones, printed with the patterns, were also 'Paisleys', and these were the most popular versions. The Paisley shawl, therefore, became an article adaptable to all pockets. This was in key with the times, because although there was much class-consciousness there was also a considerable degree of levelling, as the middle classes grew and flourished in the industrial world.

The Paisley shawl was a favourite wedding present. It was treasured by families if it was a good one. It was worn from infancy to old age. With the advent of the crinoline in the mid-1850s shawls became almost the only practical wrap that could be worn over the voluminous skirts that were generally worn and Paisley shawls were firm favourites.

From the 1870s the Paisley shawl gradually ceased to be so universally worn, suffering the fate of many fashions by becoming associated with the elderly and therefore not favoured by the young. Fabrics however, continued to be made in the Paisley pattern, and have con-tinued to be so called and to be fashionable and popular till today. In fine silks, in particular, they have been in great favour, and Paisley has remained a noted source of silk weaving from the time of her shawls.

In addition to the special Paisley type other versions of the shawl appeared. It was made in heavy wool for warmth, in bright plaids for variety; Queen Victoria had a particular liking for a shawl in tartan. In Scotland wearing of shawls practically amounted to a feminine adoption of the plaid. Long before Victoria's time Elizabeth Grant in her *Memoirs of a Highland Lady*, describing a congregation in Duthie Church in 1812 or 1813, concludes her account of the men's dress with: 'The plaid as a wrap, the plaid as a drapery, with kilt to match on some, trews on others, blue jackets on all. The women were plaided too . . . and looked

64 *The Shawl Shop of Farmer and Rogers in Regent Street, London – an 1866 advertisement shows how the shawl kept its popularity.*

among women of the lower classes as their main protection against the elements. In the early days of the present century these wearers were known to the rest of the populace of at any rate the industrial towns of Scotland as 'shawlie women'.

65 *A tailor measures a lady customer in his workroom, 1720.*

picturesquely matronly in their very high white caps. A bonnet was not to be seen, no Highland girl ever covered her head. The girls wore their hair neatly braided in front, plaited up in Grecian fashion behind . . . The wives were all in homespun, home-dyed linsey-woolsey [a linen and wool fabric] gowns, covered to the chin by the modest kerchief worn outside. The girls who could afford it had a Sabbath Day's gown of like manufacture and very bright colour . . . some had to be content with the best blue flannel petticoat and a clean white jacket, their ordinary and most becoming dress, and few of those had either shoes or stockings, but they all wore the plaid, and they folded it round them very gracefully.'

In the lowlands and in England the plaid was called the shawl, and it had an extended life

6
Doing the Sewing

The Role of Women at Home

When at the end of the seventeenth century Gregory King, one of the fathers of statistical study, picked out 'a weaver, a shoemaker and a tailor' as among the most fortunate and fully occupied of the 'handicraft labourer' class that 'hath a good trade', he touched on something very relevant to his time. Such craftsmen were irreplaceable until the machine age, which could not be anticipated in his day. The hand weaver's long reign over the loom and therefore over the production of all clothing textiles came under threat from the introduction of the first weaving machines just after the middle of the eighteenth century, when the future mass-production of materials could be visualized and the protests and attacks of weavers could do nothing to stem the march of progress. The tailor, in fact, kept his monopoly unchallenged for nearly another century, as no practical sewing machine came on the market till then, so that all stitching had to be done by hand. The sewing machine was to represent the greatest revolution in the whole history of dress.

It is difficult today to visualize a world of clothing where every stitch of every single garment or accessory had to be sewn by hand. Clothes were precious, costly even to the wealthy, the result of much time and labour being expended on every garment. So everything had to last, especially among ordinary people. Garments would be altered, refurbished, added to, re-trimmed, even adapted to new uses, eventually perhaps cut down to be worn by a child. A suit could cost as much as a considerable piece of furniture. It was also a valuable investment.

Second-hand markets for clothing existed throughout history, and the rich as well as the poor resorted to them. Clothes were also handed down from wearer to wearer, bequeathed in wills. In particular the personal servants of people of the richer classes were given the clothes of their masters and mistresses as a valued 'perk', either for their own use or that of their relatives, or to sell for profit.

The system in general meant that the discarded clothes of the rich and fashionable tended to be highly valued. They were preserved for posterity and are the mainstay of nearly all collections and exhibitions of period dress up to the last century. Ordinary garments, worn by the middle and lower classes, rarely survived. They were so much re-made, adapted, brought up to date, that actual examples are almost non-existent. Court dress and formal attire for great occasions were given a quite disproportionate amount of attention and are too often thought of as the general style in vogue at a particular time and place.

However busily tailors, and later dress-makers too, worked at making clothes, a large amount of clothing worn by all classes did not come into their range of activity. That the women of the family and the female servants should be in charge of the making and maintenance of the personal and household linen of all the members was a tradition built into the story of centuries of everyday life in England and other western countries. From their earliest days girls of all classes but the lowest were taught fine sewing and usually also embroidery and other kinds of similar handicrafts as part of their upbringing, whether or not other general and academic learning was also involved in their education. Such skills were normally exercised throughout life. From infants and children to adults, from homekeeping sons or those setting off for apprenticeships, universities or careers to daughters preparing for marriage, all looked to the home for shirts, shifts, petticoats, night clothes, handkerchiefs, neckwear, caps, cravats and a host of other accessories. It was a long time before such items became readily available in shops and markets or from travelling salesmen in quantities that bore any comparison with the vast amount produced in the home.

In a world where all sewing had to be done by hand, as was the only possible way until the middle of the nineteenth century, it seems to have been generally accepted that this mountain of sewing should be undertaken at all social levels. The Verney ladies sewed industriously, stitching shirts for their sons. Nancy Woodforde made her uncle's shirts and mended a pair of breeches. Jane Austen's characters plied their needles industriously when sitting together sociably. She herself was a notably fine sempstress and wrote happily about this activity, especially at a time when she and her sister Cassandra were busily engaged in making shirts for their brother Charles. As she wrote to Cassandra, who was away on a visit: 'When you come home you will have some shirts to make up for Charles. Mrs Davies frightened him into buying a piece of Irish linen when we were in Basingstoke.' The next year she talks of dispatching the shirts 'by half dozens as they are finished'.

When family needs had been met it was quite usual for those who could afford it to make various similar items of underwear for the poor. Mrs Delany (1700–88), of whom it is recalled that 'one of her greatest masterpieces was her own court dress, which she designed and worked in black silk' (an achievement so unusual as to be worth recording), also says of a typical ordinary day at one stage of her life, '. . . and after supper I make shirts and shifts for the poor naked wretches in the neighbourhood.'

66 *The mantua-maker, or ladies' dressmaker, emerged in the later seventeenth century and soon took over the major part of the making of women's dress. Here a fitting is shown in* The Book of English Trades, *1823.*

R. Campbell's *Complete London Tradesman* (1747) devotes a section to the Milliner, who 'though no Male Trade, has a just Claim to a Place on this Occasion, as the Fair Sex, who are generally bound to this Business, may have as much Curiosity to know the Nature of their Employment . . . as the Youth of our own Sex'. He explains: 'The Milliner is concerned in making and providing the Ladies with Linen of all sorts, fit for Wearing Apparel, from the Holland Smock to the Tippet and Commode [a kind of wired head-dress] . . . let it suffice in general that the Milliner furnished them with Holland, Cambrick, Lawn, and Lace of all sorts, and makes these Materials into Smocks, Aprons, Tippits, Handkerchiefs, Neckties, Ruffles, Mobs, Caps, Dressed-Heads, with as many *Etceteras* as would reach from *Charing Cross* to the *Royal Exchange*.'

He details much more, stresses that the milliner is a professional, and can have Paris fashion links, but adds that the milliners 'give but poor, mean Wages to every Person they employ under them' and drive their employees to debauchery and vice – in fact the first recorded cases of the sweated labour of women which was to blacken the dress trade long afterwards.

In general, not much is heard of the milliner by name in this sense after this, but the home needlewoman was supplemented considerably by women sewing for their living. In general these professionals, mainly described as mantua-makers till well into the nineteenth century, took over nearly all women's clothes-making from the man tailor, except for the seventeenth-century waistcoat, described by Sarah Fell but shortly to disappear, the riding habit and some heavy coats and wraps, which men continued to make.

The man's suit, introduced in the later seventeenth century, did more than achieve permanent domination of the male wardrobe. It also enjoyed a notable feminine influence. It was from the sixties of the seventeenth century that women began to wear what we call a riding habit – an imitation of the wide-skirted riding coat then worn by men, with a similar cravat at the neck, a periwig and cocked hat on the head but, of course, full skirts and usually many petticoats in the current fashion. Pepys, always on the scene, first saw it on 11 June 1666: 'Walking in the galleries at White Hall, I find the Ladies of honour dressed in their riding garbs, with coats and doublets with deep skirts, just, for all the world, like mine, and buttoned their doublets up the breast, with periwigs and hats, so that only for a long petticoat dragging under their men's coats, nobody could take

67 *A lady's riding habit in red woollen cloth, c.1770.*

them for women in any point whatever, which was an odde sight, and a sight which did not please me.' In spite of that, women have continued to wear such habits ever since, for a time not only for riding but for many other occasions and at many levels of society, high and low.

In Parson Woodforde's diary Mrs Custance walked over to the Parsonage in 1781 for a morning visit wearing a riding habit, and soon afterwards Nancy was given a riding habit of broadcloth by her uncle, having it made at Garths of Norwich, with a fitting on one of their visits there. This too was worn for walking and travelling. Nancy had another habit in 1793, also made at Barths, Stay and Habit Maker, of

Norwich. Nancy seems to have worn her habits for the long journeys to Somerset as well as locally for walking and when she drove herself around in what her uncle called her 'little cart'.

Two unexpected regular feminine wearers of riding habits occur in J. T. Smith's assembly of reminiscences *Book for a Rainy Day*, which though not published until 1885, is sub-titled 'Recollections of the Events of the Years 1766–1833', that is, the author's entire lifetime. His reference to the subject occurs in a description of what is to be seen around Bloomsbury and Marylebone. He describes how: 'The ground behind the north-west end of Russell Street was occupied by a farm occupied by two old maiden sisters of the name of Capper. They wore riding-habits and men's hats; one rode an old grey mare, and it was her spiteful delight to ride with a large pair of shears after boys who were flying their kites, purposely to cut their strings; the other sister's business was to seize the clothes of the lads who trespassed on their premises to bathe.'

The other territory left to the man tailor in the woman's world was that of corsetry. It was said by Campbell that these garments were made by men because the strict and tight shaping, the severe boning required to give the correct figure, called for the strength as well as the skill of the trained man tailor. The eighteenth and nineteenth centuries saw women encased in these fearsome garments in the cause of elegance, but later, easier fashion lines and the great developments in elasticized and other stretch fabrics won back this territory for the woman corset designer, even in fashionable circles. Manufacture was almost wholly a female occupation in corset factories.

From the Mantua-maker to Making Do

The dressmaker was generally called the mantua-maker in the 1700s and until well into the nineteenth century, the mantua being a looser and more casual type of dress which did not call for the strict cut and shaping which had hitherto prevailed in both men's and women's attire of any quality.

68 *Even in the nineteenth century the corset could be a daunting garment. Here a popular style is advertised in the magazine* Le Follet *in March, 1885, as being 'admirably calculated to prevent the very disagreeable occurrence of Split Seams' – presumably in the dress.*

The mantua-maker, however, varied as much as the tailor, catering for all classes. J. T. Smith, in his *Nollekens and his Times* (1828), tells an anecdote of 'one of my great-aunts, the late Mrs Hussey . . . who . . . was a fashionable sacque and mantua-maker, and lived in the Strand.' Fielding introduced her into *Tom Jones*, in which he had promised to include all his friends, as Sophia Western, 'a celebrated mantua-maker in the Strand, famous for setting off the shapes of women'. That was the top end of a trade which catered for all classes and was mainly responsible for dressing women until the age of the factory and mass-production took care of the majority – which was not fully achieved until the present century.

When Admiral Croft in Jane Austen's *Persuasion* (1816) is trying to arrange for Anne Elliot to visit his wife he assures her that the latter is 'alone, nobody but her mantua-maker with her, and they have been shut up together this half-hour, so it must be over soon'. A different kind of mantua-maker visited Nancy Woodforde. On 19 June 1797 her uncle records: 'A Mantua-Maker from Mattishall Burgh by name Burroughs came here early this Morning, and she breakfasted, dined and stayed the Afternoon at Weston Parsonage.'

The mantua-maker could have her business premises, or work in her own home, with customers calling on her, or she could go to her customer and either work there or call for discussions on style and subsequent fittings. One of her best-known rôles was that of the 'daily dressmaker', especially the choice of families of modest means in the nineteenth century, when she would work in their homes by a daily or weekly arrangement, renewing the wardrobes of the women and children for the coming season, altering and adapting, and cutting down adult garments for young people.

Whatever the period, it was usual for the customer to buy the actual materials, trimmings and dress accessories. That is probably why so often in memoirs and literature in general the constant references to buying a gown meant in fact buying the material with which it should be made up. Purchases could be made in shops, from general drapers, mercers, and haberdashers, all of whom had been a feature of London and some larger towns for more than two centuries, offering various degrees of choice ranging from woollen materials to specialized varieties of silks, muslins and linens. In villages purchases would probably be made from travelling salesmen, as Parson Woodforde records, by the salesman either calling at the door or setting himself up at local market days or fairs where he would be plying

69 *Simpler styles of dress for a time, a series of designs drawn in 1823.*

his trade. As towns grew from the later eighteenth century village shops became more widespread and their range of goods extended to textiles in some cases. There was also a lot of purchasing done by people visiting London or the big towns and buying for friends at home.

As paper patterns did not become generally available to the public until well into the nineteenth century the cutting out of garments according to the customer's wishes or from an existing garment also fell largely on the mantua-maker or dressmaker. In the days before factory production existed she could develop quite a considerable business, employing staff, training apprentices and becoming a considerable force in the dress of women at many levels of society.

Although magazines became one of the most popular ways of spreading news about dress among ordinary women, this was not evident when they first began to appear in England, about 1750. They were originally aimed at the intellectual woman, not the fashionable few or would-be-fashionable multitude. Not until the very end of the eighteenth century did Heideloff's *Gallery of Fashion*, which appeared from 1794 to 1803, give the reader a publication devoted entirely to fashion. Even so, it was an expensively produced monthly, the first to have coloured illustrations, which consisted of two plates each month, with full descriptions of the models shown. The plates were, of course, hand-coloured, as colour printing was a remote dream, with metallic paints for the parts of the attire which were of gold, silver or other metals. The writings of the time show that ordinary country women were still acquiring their knowledge of dress from hearsay, from visitors to London or Bath, or by copying each other. Jane Austen shows this in her novels.

Fashion magazines became more numerous throughout the nineteenth century, but they tended to concentrate on high fashion. Thus Ackermann's elaborately named *Repository of Arts, Literature, Commerce, Manufactures, Fashion and Politics*, which appeared monthly from 1809 to 1828 and in its last year, 1829, was called *Ackermann's Repository of Fashion*, was a high-style arts publication and dealt with high fashion, not with what the majority of people wore. The 450 fashion plates included in it were elaborate and luxurious.

Changing days and ways did not unduly disturb all women. Sometimes such problems could be set aside, even if money were short and fashion an interesting topic. This was what happened to the ladies of Cranford, the early Victorian small town immortalized by Mrs Gaskell in her story of 1851. Their appearance was indeed important to them, but clothes were not much talked of because 'none of us spoke of money, because the subject savoured of commerce and trade, and though some might be poor, we were all aristocratic'. That is, they were not in 'trade' – a long-standing social distinction which persisted to some extent into the present century.

Bonnets were the main item to receive attention in Cranford – they were more affordable than larger articles of wear. For a funeral 'Miss Jenkyns sent out for a yard of black crape, and employed herself busily in trimming the little black bonnet' previously mentioned. When the accepted visiting hour of noon arrives the ladies did not change dresses, but bonnets. When an unduly early visitor arrives, 'Miss Matty had not changed the cap with yellow ribbons that had been Miss Jenkyns' best and which Miss Matty was now wearing out in private, putting on the one made in imitation of Mrs Jamieson's at all times when she expected to be seen'. She slipped away to change it, but in a fluster put the new cap on top of the old and reappeared all unconscious of doing so and 'looked at us with bland satisfaction'. On another occasion an early visitor provoked the same wish 'to change caps and collars'.

Caps were important at Cranford. Two sisters, ex-ladies' maids, set up as milliners with their savings, were patronized by local ladies and scored a business success there: 'Lady Arley, for instance, would occasionally give Miss Barkers the pattern of an old cap of hers, which they immediately copied and circulated

70 *How the ordinary man dressed in the seventeenth century. An auction sale at Garraways Coffee House in 1671.*

among the *élite* of Cranford. I say the *élite*, for Miss Barkers had caught the trick of the place, and piqued themselves upon their aristocratic connection. They would not sell their caps and ribbons to anyone without a pedigree.' Farmers' wives and such like were turned away and had to resort to 'the universal shop, where the profits of brown soap and moist sugar enabled the proprietor to go straight to ... London where, as he often told his customers, Queen Adelaide had appeared only the very week before in a cap exactly like the one he showed them ... and had been complimented by King William on the becoming nature of her head-dress'.

A further enhancement of the cap was the wearing over it of a calash, that is 'a covering worn over caps, not unlike the heads fastened on old-fashioned gigs ... This kind of headgear always made an awful impression on the children in Cranford'. For a special party a new cap would be brought out or even bought, as when Miss Pole 'lectured dear Miss Matty' and 'absolutely ended by assuring her it was her duty ... to buy a new cap and go to the party'. For another party Miss Matty explains that 'she was, perhaps, too old to care about dress, but a new cap she must have; and, having heard that turbans were worn', she wants guidance on that too.

A fashion show at Cranford, held by the local shopkeeper, is a big event, to which Miss Matty goes eagerly 'to see exactly how my new silk gown must be made', 'anticipating the sight of the glossy fold' of silk on the counter 'with as much delight as if the five sovereigns set apart for the purchase could buy all the silks in the shop'. Owing to a sad turn of events, it was the dress that never was, and thus the fashion show is not described in the detail one would have enjoyed.

There is not much mention of knitting and sewing in Cranford, though there are indications that these were not neglected. The narrator of the book records that there was in that quiet life 'all the more time for me to hear old-world stories from Miss Pole while she sat knitting, and I making my father's shirts. I always took a quantity of plain sewing to Cranford, for, as we did not read or walk much, I found it a capital time to get through my work'. New knitting stitches 'help to set up a kind of intimacy' between two Cranford ladies. Miss Matty is also described as 'sitting ... much as usual, she in the blue chintz easy chair, with her back to the light and her knitting in her hand'.

One main problem of women of the time occurs on one occasion, when the possible need to earn money arises. The victim of a sudden loss of income considers 'her qualifications for earning money. "I can sew neatly," said she, "and I like nursing. I think, too, I could manage a house, if anyone would try me as housekeeper, or I would go into a shop as saleswoman, if they would have patience with me at first."' When Miss Matty is faced with this problem, 'the education common to ladies fifty years ago' rules out teaching and leaves little but 'making candle-lighters, or "spills" (as she preferred calling them) ... and knitting garters in a variety of dainty stitches', and there was little scope there.

The Reaction Against Home Sewing
The amount of sewing done at home by a large proportion of women all through the centuries before the sewing machine became a practical invention was generally unavoidable. Where the family's means were limited it was the practical, economical way of providing underwear, accessories, household linen, often some outer garments too. Patching and mending likewise were necessary. Sewing was also to

many women an agreeable occupation, whether or not they needed to do it. The lighter kind of stitching and embroidery was an accompaniment of social life, and remained so to some extent after the sewing machine appeared.

Often, however, it was tedious and oppressive. Not all women enjoy sewing. A bright window is opened into the early nineteenth century by the chance preservation and publication of some of the diaries kept by an obscure North Country woman, Ellen Weeton. *Miss Weeton's Journal of a Governess* deals with ordinary dress from various points of view. There is her own outfit when she goes mountaineering alone in the Isle of Man in 1812: 'A lonely female ... for I had on a small slouch straw hat, a grey stuff jacket, and petticoat [still an outer garment], a white net bag in one hand, and a parasol in the other.' Later '2 gowns, a black and a grey sarsenet [a silk material], a muff and tippet, and a marone velvet, were left to me by my aunt'. Still later, unhappily married: 'Cloaths I could not procure, unless I got them on credit.' But most interesting is her commentary on the housewife's traditional rôle of endless mending and patching and her own revolt against sewing when she was separated from her husband. Thus in Wales, she meditates: 'I have, for some years, entirely given up all kinds of needlework which has no real utility to recommend it. I do not say anything in condemnation of ornamental needlework, although I could say much, and I think justly ... When I sew it is to make necessary clothing, and to keep it in repair ... It is so little of an amusement to me, that were I rich enough, I should employ others to do it, for I think it is a duty in the affluent female to let others live. I do not look upon it as a merit for any young person to make her own dresses, bonnets, shoes, or lace, if she be rich. I *do* consider it a merit that she should be *able* to make them, for no one so affluent but may suffer a reverse, and every female should know how to earn a living.'

That home sewing by those who did not need to do it for economic reasons was not a virtue but on the contrary a disservice to those of their sex who needed to sew to make a living was a point that does not seem to have occurred or at least to have been voiced publicly until the nineteenth century. It was made strongly by Mary Lamb in her only known writing for grown-up people, an article which appeared in the April 1815 issue of the *British Lady's Magazine*, a short-lived monthly publication which aimed at taking a more serious view of women's activities than was usual at the time. She treats the subject of sewing and all kinds of needlework 'not as an art, but as a factor in social life', as her biographer Anne Gilchrist says, continuing: 'She pleads both for the sake of the bodily welfare of the many thousands of women who have to earn their bread by it, and of the mental well-being of those who have not so to do, that it should be regarded, like any other mechanical art, as a thing to be done for hire; and that what a woman *does* work at should be real work, something, that is, which yields a return either of mental or of pecuniary profit.'

In what is a sagacious forecast of the future course of women's employment problems Mary Lamb points out that she speaks from personal experience: 'In early life I passed eleven years in the exercise of my needle for a livelihood.' Now she sees that 'women have, of late, been rapidly advancing in intellectual improvement', but there is one great obstacle in the way. 'Needle-work and intellectual improvement are naturally in a state of warfare,' she urges, and 'I affirm that I know not a single family where there is not some essential drawback to its comfort which may be traced to needle-work *done at home*, as the phrase is for all needle-work performed in a family by some of its own members, and for which no remuneration in money is received or expected.' The woman who does such sewing and does not need to is robbing needy women and should have 'contributed her part to the slender means of the corset-maker, the milliner, the dressmaker, the plain worker, the embroidress and all the numerous classifications of females supporting themselves by *needle-work*, that great staple commodity which is alone appropriated to the self supporting part of our sex.'

'Home sewing,' she continues, 'should be assessed as part of the family income' and 'it might be a laudable scruple of conscience, and no bad test to herself of her own motive, if a lady who had no absolute need were to give the money so saved to poor needle-women belonging to those branches of employment from which she has borrowed these shares of pleasurable labour.'

When she wrote thus Mary could not know that from mid-century factory production and, above all, the introduction of the sewing machine, were to bring to an end this era of endless home sewing. Ordinary people were the first to feel the change, for inexpensive machine-made shirts and underwear were among the first parts of the wardrobe to feel the effects, good and bad, of the change.

Unfortunately, however, what looked like being an age of plenty, of abundant inexpensive clothing, turned out to be an age too of sweated labour, of underpaid, overworked factory conditions which pressed most heavily on the women who formed the main part of the clothing industry's workers.

Nor was Mary Lamb to know that the nineteenth-century social conscience, stirred as never before by overwork and underpayment, and by the plight of the poor who had to accept such oppression, would be centred time and again upon the sufferings of girls and women toiling at sewing, making clothes for the rich and heedless.

Girls are depicted, like dressmaker Mary Barton in Mrs Gaskell's novel of that title (1848), toiling over making mourning 'for Mrs Ogden as keeps the greengrocer's shop in Oxford Road'. She overworks because of the urgency of mourning clothes, still hand-sewn, because that was 1848. In the same author's *Ruth* (1853), late at night 'more than a dozen girls still sat in the room ... stitching away as if for very life ... not daring to gape or show any manifestation of sleepiness ... They knew that,

stay up as late as they might, the work-hours of the next day must begin at eight, and their young limbs were very weary.' Ruth, a new apprentice, meditates: 'Oh! how shall I ever get through five years of these terrible nights in the close room and in that oppressive stillness which lets every sound of the thread be heard as it goes eternally backwards and forwards.' That was making dresses for a ball in the Assembly Rooms.

Most famous of all, Hood's *The Song of the Shirt*, encapsulates every imaginable soul-destroying misery of the impoverished, over-worked seamstress, hand-sewing in 1843, when it first appeared in the Christmas number of *Punch*. The same miseries continued too for the children toiling in mines and factories, whose victimization was the subject of attention and vehement protest on the part of both writers and general public alike.

71 *Dressmaking to earn a living: a grim cartoon by Leech, 1849, as the result of a case in the Metropolitan Police Court which revealed that women were being paid one-and-a-half pence for making a complete shirt. A companion picture –* Pin Money– *showed the wealthy woman sewing as a hobby.*

72 *Sweated labour: a homeworker of the 1850s.*

Secondhand Clothing

Secondhand – by which we also mean third-, fourth-, fifth- and in fact any-hand – clothing, from the very earliest times to the rise of mass-manufacture in the present century played a major part in the dress scene, and not only for poor people. Its roots were in the barter system, the earliest trading of all, then followed pedlars and then the whole gamut of shops and markets of all kinds.

By the seventeenth century, the start of the period now being considered, the secondhand market was important, and used by most classes. Clothes were both expensive and very laborious to produce, so they were not lightly discarded. Ben Jonson advised young men possessed of some land and coming to London to seek their fortune that ''twere good you turned four or five acres of your best land into two or three trunks of apparel,' because appearance counted for much. Good clothes could also, he pointed out, be a very marketable and profitable commodity. The well-born Verneys sold and bought in the secondhand market. It was customary for the well-off to give discarded clothes to valued servants, to leave their clothes to such employees in their wills. Sarah, Duchess of Marlborough, left half her wardrobe to her personal maid, the rest to two other women servants. Such servants often wanted to sell their bequests, not wear them – like Richardson's Pamela, who had risen too successfully in life to want them for herself.

This trade was well-established in London. It grew still more in the eighteenth century. Specific areas concentrated on it, as on other categories of dress. The immediate vicinity of Houndsditch, on the east side of the City, was one such area. Another favourite district was round Seven Dials, with Monmouth Street the most famous name, recorded by Dickens. Here the honours were shared between secondhand shops and pawnshops. Nearby was the developing shopping area of Covent Garden, part of the westward trend of fashion in London. Rosemary Lane was popularly known as Rag Fair, and was, on the contrary, near the Tower.

73 *Doing business in Rosemary Lane, prominent in the secondhand trade. An illustration from Mayhew's* London Labour and the London Poor, *1851.*

The secondhand clothier, known as a clothes broker, was a respectable tradesman, included in Campbell's *Complete London Tradesman* as being skilled in tailoring, taking apprentices and needing capital to set up in business. The pawnbroker came into a different category, but always, as even now, a necessary one.

The giving of personal clothes to their servants by the better off was a practice which continued up to the present century, and was a recognized part of domestic life. Such clothes, disposed of to the clothes broker, became a quite important means by which a fairly humble man could present a well-dressed appearance at a cost within his means. When Samuel and Sarah Adams wrote their *The Complete Servant* (1825), one of the earliest books on the subject, stating that they had been for '50 years servants in different families', they included among the 'perks' of butler and valet the master's cast-off clothes. That women servants should fare likewise is voiced in advice to the employer in one of the many eighteenth-century 'guides to right living', which were popular reading at the time: 'Your care must not stop at your Children, let it reach your menial Servants; though you are their Master, you are also their Father.'

In the early part of the nineteenth century the secondhand clothes trade grew by leaps and bounds. The population was increasing, mainly due to improvements in health and sanitation. As industry grew people moved to the new factory areas and to London from rural districts where the old cottage industries and domestic pattern of work were going into eclipse. Though spinning and weaving could now be carried out mechanically, there was until the mid-1850s no satisfactory sewing machine, so all clothing still had to be made by hand. The poor no longer had time to contrive clothes, gifts from local gentry did not exist in towns, and the value of second-hand clothing was therefore high. Nor was it only the poor who sought it out.

A vivid and detailed account of the second-hand clothes trade of the mid-nineteenth century is given by that generous philanthropist, journalist and pioneer sociologist, Henry Mayhew, in his *London Labour and the London Poor*, first published in 1851 and, though reissued in the early 1860s with many additions, unduly neglected in more recent times. Dramatist, novelist, biographer, travel writer and joint-editor of *Punch* in its first days, Mayhew, in his study of the working poor of London, produced a new *genre* of literature. The twenty-odd pages devoted to the secondhand clothes trades show at their best his sharp observation, vivid descriptive talents, intense humanity and mastery of every kind of detail.

The size of the secondhand clothes market which Mayhew surveys is astonishing – but it was called for in a Greater London which had increased its population from 865,000 to 1,500,000 between 1800 and 1830 and added on another million people from then until 1850, as Peter Quennell records in his edition of *Mayhew*. In those millions were included all degrees

74 *A poor woman, shown in Mayhew.*

of poverty and privation as well as massive Victorian wealth and prosperity. To his particular area Mayhew brings qualities which lead Peter Quennell to compare him with Defoe for grasp of fact and detail, observation and a kind of poetic insight into humanity, though 'it would be presumptuous, no doubt, to call him the nineteenth century Defoe'.

First then, for some of Mayhew's facts. 'The great mart of second-hand apparel was, in the last century, in Monmouth-street; now ... termed Dudley-street, Seven Dials ... Now Monmouth-street, for its new name is hardly legitimised, has no finery. Its second-hand wares are almost wholly confined to old boots and shoes ... A little business is carried on in second-hand apparel ... but it is insignificant. The head-quarters of this second-hand trade are now in Petticoat and Rosemary lanes, especially in Petticoat lane, and the traffic there carried on may be called enormous ... But the business in Petticoat and Rosemary lanes is mostly of a retail character.'

This is because of a new phenomenon – the Old Clothes Exchange dealing with the wholesale side, 'and it is rather remarkable that a business occupying so many persons, and requiring such facilities for examination and arrangement, should not until the year 1843 have had its regulated proceedings'. This, Mayhew suggests, coincides with an increase in business in secondhand clothing which cannot be equalled by any other trade. The Clothes Exchange operates in a honeycomb of streets in the old clothes area of East London and carries on also large-scale business in exports, mainly to Ireland, Holland and Belgium.

75 *Another London type, from Mayhew. Note the top hat, worn by all classes.*

The retail markets nearby are patronized by 'anyone – shop-keeper, artisan, clerk, costermonger, or gentleman'. Mayhew pauses to reflect on the story behind the clothes; 'in what scenes of gaiety or gravity, in the opera house, or the senate, had the perhaps departed wearers of some of that heap of old clothes figured – through how many possessors, and again through what new scenes of middle-class or artisan comfort had these dresses passed.'

Some, on the other hand, are 'garments originally made for the labouring classes. These are made up of every description of colour and materials – cloth, corduroy, woollen cords, fustian, moleskin, flannel, velveteen, plaids . . . In them are to be seen coats, great-coats, jackets, trousers, and breeches, but no other habiliments.' The trade of the central market is authoritatively said to be £1,500 a week all the year round.

In Petticoat Lane the goods offered include 'decent, frowsy, half-rotten, or smart and good habiliments'. All have passed through the Exchange or central market and 'been made ready for use'. Although there are some other traders in and around Petticoat Lane, it 'is essentially the old-clothes district, and . . . there is perhaps between two and three miles of old clothes', presenting 'a vista of many coloured garments, alike on the sides and on the ground', solid with clothes: 'Dress coats, frock coats, great coats, livery and game-keepers' coats, paletots, tunics, trousers, knee-breeches, waistcoats, capes, pilot coats, working jackets, plaids, hats, dressing gowns, shirts, Guernsey frocks, are all displayed . . . mixed with the hues of the women's garments, spotted and striped.' Plus boots, handkerchiefs, lace and muslins, hats, 'while, incessantly threading their way through all this intricacy, is a mass of people, some of whose dresses speak of recent purchases in the lane'.

Rosemary Lane is similar, but only three-quarters of a mile long, without the 'strongly marked peculiarities' of Petticoat Lane, but surrounded by similar streets, round Dockland and the Minories. It is a jam-packed hotch-

76 *A feature of London streets was the coffee stall, again shown by Mayhew in* London Labour and the London Poor.

potch of goods, from old boots to new lace and muslin, plus old metal and glass, furniture, toys, ornaments. A street seller of men's clothes says that frock coats are best sellers, bob-tailed coats (dress coats) unpopular. 'Some buyers are poor, but genteel people buys such things as fancy weskits ... O, there's ladies comes here for a bargain, I can tell you, and gentlemen too.'

There is a wealth of detail about this trade, and some reflections too, on the very poor customers: 'Whether the state of things in which an industrious widow, or a lot of industrious persons, can spare only 1d for a child's clothing (and nothing, perhaps, for their own) is to be lauded in a Christian country, is another question, fraught with grave political and social considerations.'

The coming age of mass-produced factory clothes could not yet be foreseen, but it would not solve these problems, at least for many years to come. But as that future trade was largely built up by Jewish immigrants who came to Britain in great numbers in the 1880s because of pogroms in Eastern Europe, it is perhaps worth noting that before that time Henry Mayhew had devoted special attention to Jewish street-buyers, pointing out that 'during the eighteenth century, the popular feeling ran very high against the Jews, although to the masses they were almost strangers, except as men employed in the not-very-formidable occupation of collecting and vending second-hand clothes. The old feeling against them seems to have lingered among the English people, and their own greed in many instances engendered further dislike. By Mayhew's time the Jews had diversified into many occupations, many of them in imports, from watches and jewellery to fruit and tobacco, but Mayhew assigns them a place in Petticoat Lane and prominence in the Houndsditch and Minories areas as shopkeepers, warehousemen and manufacturers. There were still many of them working as secondhand clothes men, buying old clothes door-to-door or in the streets, or bartering them for other secondhand goods, and selling them in Petticoat Lane. Mayhew estimates that there were from 5,000 to 6,000 such old-clothes men in London in his time.

The fact that jumble sales are one of the regular minor events of daily life today is evidence that the gravity with which second-hand clothing was regarded for centuries has passed away. Mass production of clothing, of all types, the various amenities of the welfare state, social security and the social services have all contributed to a changed attitude to dress.

The first record of jumble sales is given as 1898 in the Oxford English Dictionary. They flourished from then and speedily became an accepted part of town and country life alike. They were and are an important means of fundraising for all kinds of charities, widely advertised in local papers and shop windows, and for the middle classes they are a main means of disposing of clothes not worn out but outmoded or for some reason no longer wanted. 'Nearly New' and charity shops have added to the story of clothes disposal – and acquirement.

The last old clothes dealer in London's Rag Fair closed down in 1874 owing to lack of business. But paradoxically certain second-hand clothes can today fetch huge prices, up to hundreds and even thousands of pounds, at London's main auction rooms, where they have become valuable 'antiques'. They are competed for by museums and at times worn proudly by adventurous leaders of fashion.

7
Cleaning and Dyeing

Washing Day

For centuries 'washing day' hung like a dark cloud over most households. To the majority of today's younger generation the very term is probably meaningless, but it took the automatic washing machine to oust it and for most ordinary people in Britain that peerless invention did not come into everyday life until the 1960s. Although pioneered in a crude form in the USA in the first decade of this century, it did not appear even there in anything like its modern form until the late 1920s. A trickle of US machines then began to come into Britain at a high price, but the first steps towards bringing the automatic washing machine into general use date from the 1950s.

Until then Black Monday figured strongly in the household calendar, but the idea of washing day as a weekly ritual was a nineteenth-century one. Prior to that washing day had been much less frequent, in the seventeenth century often coming only four or five times a year and in the eighteenth century usually at intervals of five or six weeks.

This is at once odd and very natural. With clothes costly, precious and laborious to make it would seem sensible to take care of them by seeing that they were kept as clean as possible. But many more garments than now were made of materials which could not be washed, including coveted and costly silks, satins, velvets and brocades. Moreover, the process of washing was extremely complicated and difficult, and to some extent presented problems until the present century.

The elementary way of washing clothes – in the nearest river, rubbing them clean against stones or sand, and spreading them out to dry on rocks or bushes in the sunshine and wind – was only a partial and very optimistic solution. To the majority of people by the seventeenth century the process would have to be carried out in the family kitchen or backyard. Water would have to be fetched by hand from well or standpipe, heated in cauldrons on a fire, probably of wood, on a brick base. The water would have to be transferred to tubs, the process often involving many repetitions. More water would be needed for rinsing. Space for drying could be a problem, especially in bad weather.

All this meant a considerable family upheaval. Sarah Fell notes in her accounts the employing and paying of two extra people for washing days every few months. Not even Samuel Pepys could take the matter philosophically in his London home. He found the business very distasteful, as he described it on 11 January 1661. It started with his being 'waked this morning at 4 o'clock by my wife to call the maids to their wash'. Though he escaped to his office during the day he came home at night to find 'the house foul with the washing and quite out of order against tomorrow's dinner'.

Parson Woodforde is less perturbed, but notes with relief on 7 March 1791: 'Washing week at our House, and a fine day.' He gives a detailed account of how the process went in that house, a normal, middle-class one of the day. Thus on 10 June 1799, he says: 'Washing Week with us this Week. We wash every five weeks. Our present Washerwomen are Anne Downing and Anne Richmond. Washing and Ironing generally take us Four Days. The Washerwomen breakfast and dine the Monday and

77 *The problems of fetching water for washing clothes in early days could be very acute. From Tempest's* Cries of London *(1666–1702).*

Tuesday and have each one Shilling on their going away in the evening of Tuesday.' In accordance with his habits, he is quick to show his appreciation of their work by making them a present of a gaily coloured handkerchief apiece.

He is not unduly disturbed by the event, receives visitors, dines at home. Other washing days are merely noted. Ironing appears to be undertaken by the household, with the two servant maids in charge, but on 1 June 1800 he notes: 'Nancy, very busy most of the Morning, in Ironing her Clothes in our Kitchen.' Weather and ironing also were important to Sara Hutchinson who, in a letter of autumn 1810 says: 'This has been an ironing day. We thought ourselves lucky to get the clothes dried in this broken weather.'

Surprisingly, one of the fullest accounts of the old-style washing day is given in *Lark Rise to Candleford*, Flora Thompson's absorbing saga of humble village life in the 1880s at Juniper Hill, the Oxfordshire village of her childhood: 'Monday was washing-day, and then the place fairly hummed with activity. "What d'ye think of the weather?" "Shall we get 'em dry?" were the questions shouted across gardens, or asked as the women met going to and from the well for water. There was no gossiping at corners that morning. It was before the days of patent soaps and washing powders, and much hard rubbing was involved. There were no washing coppers, and the clothes had to be boiled in the big cooking pots over the fire. Often these inadequate vessels would boil over and fill the house with steam ... tempers grew short and nerves frayed long before the clothes, well blued, were hung on the lines or spread on the hedges. In wet weather they had to be dried indoors, and no-one who has not experienced it can imagine the misery of living for several days with a firmament of drying clothes or lines overhead.'

Washing day could spill over into the rest of the week. Tess, in Hardy's *Tess of the D'Urbervilles*, comes home one evening to find 'her mother amid the group of children, as Tess had left her, hanging over the Monday washing-tub, which had now, as always, lingered on to the end of the week'.

The chief washing-day problem of the past was one which to people of today, old and young in this case, seems an unlikely one, surrounded as we are with every imaginable kind of soap and detergent. It was simply that of what to clean the clothes with.

Various cleaning agents were devised from very early times. One of the most usual, employed in classical times in countries round the Mediterranean, was fuller's earth dissolved with an alkaline solution, such as water poured through wood or with urine added to it. This was known as lye and it provided the basis of the earliest soaps, the invention of which is usually ascribed to the Phoenicians and believed to have been passed on to the Gauls and thereby to other parts of Western Europe. The addition of animal or vegetable fats or oils to a lye produced a solid or semi-solid substance after being boiled and left to cool and thicken, resulting in a manageable substance which would absorb dirt and grease.

This process continued, with variations in the kinds of oils and alkalis employed, through most of recorded history. A soap factory has been excavated at Pompeii. In luxurious societies perfumes were added to enhance the attractions of soap for toilet use. It remained an expensive luxury when manufactured commercially, and most everyday households continued to make their own into the early part of the last century.

How little soap-making changed is illustrated by the detailed account of it given by R. Campbell in his *Complete London Tradesman*, published in 1747. Surveying more than 300 trades then practised in eighteenth-century London, it gives very much the traditional 'composition of Soap'. It says: 'Soap is composed of Lime, Salt of Vegetables and the Fat of Animals; a Lee or Lixivium is made of Kelp, that is, the salt of Sea Weed obtained by burning, or of the White Ashes of other Vegetables, into which is added a Quantity of Lime-water. When the Lee has stood long enough in the Fatts to extract all the Salts from the Ashes, it is then drained off and put into a Boiler, with a Proportion of Tallow, (if for hard Soap) or of Oil (if for soft Soap), where it is allowed to boil until the Tallow, or Oil is sufficiently incorporated with the strong Lee, and is become of one thick Consistence; it is then taken out with Ladles and poured into Chests, before it is cool they pour over it some Blue, which penetrates through the Mass when it is cold, it is taken out of the Chests, and cut into Lengths with a Wire, and laid up to dry; it is a laborious nasty Business, but abundantly profitable and requires no great Share of Ingenuity; if the Master and one Man in the House understands the Business, the whole Work may be performed by Labourers.'

The home manufacture of soap continued through the seventeenth and eighteenth centuries to be the general practice of ordinary people because British commercial production was mainly for commercial users and because heavy taxation was imposed on imported soap from European countries. Rendered-down animal fats and home-made lye with wood-ash were still used and the laborious nature of the process and the unattractive, unpleasant-smelling results probably helped to account for the rarity of washing days and perhaps also for the general dislike of washing and bathing.

It was not until the end of the eighteenth century that substantial progress towards the production of commercially made soaps of an attractive kind for the ordinary household, for personal use as well as for the family washing day, was made as a result of the researches of chemists into the constituents of oils and fats. Two Frenchmen were pioneers in this, Nicholas Leblanc (1742–1806) and Michel Eugène Chevreul (1786–1889). The large-scale use of manufactured soaps in the home and the abandonment of domestic soap-making were, however, nineteenth-century achievements.

The great leap forward in soap-making and the development of washing agents in Britain were the achievements of William Hesketh Lever, later Lord Leverhulme (1851–1925).

Until well through the nineteenth century soap was still being shredded and mixed with soda at home to produce soap flakes suitable for household clothes washing. A soap powder came on the market in the 1860s. Lux soap flakes were introduced in 1900 and other soap powders followed fast upon that. It was, however, not until the Second World War that the synthetic or soapless detergent now generally used was produced on a large scale. The shortage of animal fats and oils gave a stimulus to research into cleaning agents based on oil or by-products of coal. These were in fact superior in cleansing power to ordinary soaps, because their molecular structure reduced the surface tension of the water and increased its potency as a cleaner. Biological detergents, developed in the 1960s, have an additional potency as stain removers which is a great asset in laundering.

A CHEERFUL OLD SOUL.

IT is possible for a woman **with increasing years** to continue to do laundry work. **Thousands** who would have been laid aside under the old system of washing **have proved what "SUNLIGHT SOAP" can do** in reducing labour. The cleansing properties of **"SUNLIGHT SOAP"** save years **of arduous toil.** Reader, prove **"SUNLIGHT SOAP"** for yourself, as by giving the best article a trial you will do yourself a real service.

SUNLIGHT SOAP MONTHLY COMPETITION
PRIZES VALUE OVER £600.

FOR YOUNG FOLKS ONLY. Competitors not to be over 17 years of age last birthday.

The first of these Monthly Competitions commenced on August 31, and will be followed by others until further notice.

There is no element of chance in these Competitions, the winning of a prize depending entirely on the perseverance and trouble taken to collect the wrappers. The Competitions are held every month, so failure in one does not discourage but stimulates to a fresh effort.

PRIZES VALUE OVER £600.—60 Silver Keyless Lever Watches, value £4 4s. each.
100 Silver Keyless Watches, value 30s. each. 8 Tricycles and 8 Safety Bicycles.

EXTRA PRIZES.—Unsuccessful competitors who have sent in not less than 24 "Coupons" will receive, free of cost and postage paid, a *facsimile* reproduction (size 16½ inches by 11½ inches) of the painting by W. P. FRITH, R.A., exhibited in the Royal Academy, 1889, and named by us "So Clean." The *Daily Telegraph*, July 11, 1889, says of it—"A charming little picture:" When this picture is out of print others will take its place.

Names of Winners of each month's Competition will be advertised in "Tit Bits" and "Answers" the fourth week of the month following.

☞ Send full **Name** and **Address** on Postcard for Rules to LEVER BROS., Ltd., Port Sunlight, near Birkenhead.

Purchasers, see that you get a Sunlight Soap Wrapper with each Tablet.

78 *One of Lord Leverhulme's major contributions to easing the burden of washing day: an advertisement of 1890.*

Gadgets to help the housewife with the sheer toil of clothes washing were developed only slowly, and were usually either very basic or else expensive and available only to the wealthy. For ordinary people various kinds of dolly sticks helped to save some of the toil. Their purpose was to aerate the washing in the tub by pounding it up and down in the soapy solution. They were used widely in the nineteenth century. The other gadget most commonly seen in the ordinary home was a washing board, a wooden board with a corrugated zinc surface on which the clothes were rubbed to remove dirt. Another practical aid which won wide popularity among ordinary people was the hand-wringer, attached to a table or washtub with clamps and adjusted so as to drive excess water out of washed items. The large mangle, originally meant to press such items as sheets, was also used as this kind of dryer, but needed more space, such as the cellar of a suburban or quite modest country house. When there was no space for a separate washroom or scullery there was often a wash-boiler consisting of a cauldron, at first of cast-iron, but later of copper (from which it got its usual name), set in a brick or stone outer case, with space for a fire underneath. This became popular in the middle and later nineteenth century and early twentieth century in middle-class homes. Various early washing machines, manually operated, were introduced, but were usually costly and bulky and had only a limited appeal.

Ordinary kitchens from the past rarely survive any more than do ordinary clothes, but one in the Georgian House in Bristol (c. 1790) contains a number of contemporary washing aids which, though beyond the means of the mass of people, are realistic enough to illustrate the kind of ideas available at a price not wholly prohibitive. The spacious laundry of the country house of Errdig, in Clwyd, is obviously that of a family of wealth and status, but it is an absorbing subject for study. Constructed in

79 *Aids to washing in the nineteenth century: wooden dolly sticks to aerate the washing and wooden washing-board with zinc corrugated rubbing surface, all from Dawlish Museum Society.*

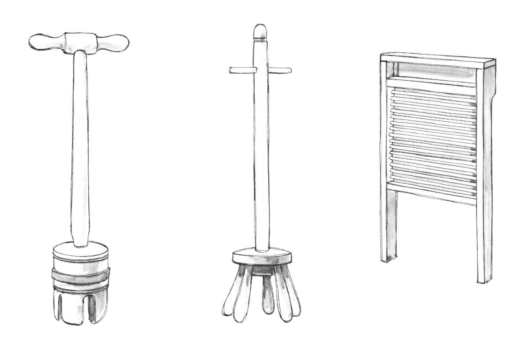

"Vowel" E6.   Capacity 15 shirts, 27in. by 6in.
              Brass Capped Rollers £22 0 0
              (AS ILLUSTRATED.)

80 *A successful early washing-machine:
Thomas Bradford's rotary washing-machine,
introduced in the 1850s; a circular drum rotates
inside the octagonal outer case and is turned by
hand by means of a handle on the smaller wheel.
The large wheel wrings and mangles the wash and
15 shirts can be dealt with at a time.*

1770 and maintained with all its original features and equipment, it consists of a wet
laundry and a dry laundry, enabling the processes to be kept apart. It was recently featured
in a book *The Servants' Hall*, a domestic history
of that house.

Mrs Beeton, still regarded as the *doyenne* of
advisors on how a home should be run, gives a
detailed account of how to deal with the
laundry of a small household, consisting only of
parents and one baby, in the latter part of the
nineteenth century in the *Housewife's Treasury
of Domestic Information*. It was for long in
popular demand, like her other works. She
advises Tuesday, not Monday, as washing day,
because Monday tends to be extra busy after
the weekend. But on Monday the clothes are to
be looked over, sorted and soaked, the copper
filled, the copper fire lighted in readiness. She
recommends a small washing machine, which
she says should cost £2 or £3 and which suitably
'would be Harper's Twelvetrees "Villa" Invention'. The washing agent should be 'that well
known now almost all over the world as Extract
of Soap, or rather, to give it its full title,
"concentrated extract of soap"'.

In her 'simple and easily followed directions'
she devotes ten pages to 'The Whole Art of
Washing', with details about the handling of
every imaginable problem, from stains and
scorching to children's striped socks and black
lace. There are twelve more pages on ironing,
dyeing, renovating feathers and mending a
variety of items. Washing was still a formidable
undertaking.

Early clothing fabrics were not fine enough to
call for ironing and it was not until the seventeenth century that domestic irons were first
made in Britain, usually of iron or steel. The
tailor's 'goose' was much older, but clothes of
his workmanship would not normally be
washed at home – or anywhere else in most
cases. There were two main types of household
iron. The box iron was a hollow container into
which was inserted a unit heated in the fire or on
the stove. This was called a slug and there were
normally two, one being heated or re-heated
while the other was being used. The other type
of iron was a solid one, usually made of cast iron
and called the flat-iron or, oddly, the sad iron –
'sad' here being a synonym for solid or heavy. In
this case the whole iron was heated on fire or
stove, and again two were normally in use for an
ironing. Both types of iron were alike in design,
pointed in front and widening to a flat back. The
sizes varied, and the flat iron was the longest to

81 *Not till the 1920s did the electric washing-
machine begin to come within the means of many
households, when such smiling advertisements as
this began to appear.*

Washing day

HOW often have you been inconvenienced in this way?

You have probably prepared your whole week's washing, got the water in the copper boiling, baths ready, and everything waiting for the arrival of the washerwoman, when you get the above message—"Mother cannot come to-day."

There is no need for a washerwoman if you use a Western Electric guaranteed clothes washer and wringer. The whole of your week's washing can be done by electricity in much less time and with greater efficiency at a cost of approximately one penny per hour.

The wringer works by electricity too, so that there is no hard work left for you to do.

Ask your dealer for particulars, or write direct to us. Demonstrations given daily in our Modern Kitchen at Connaught House, Aldwych, W.C.

Western Electric
WASHING MACHINE.

82 *The £2 or £3 washing machine recommended by Beeton's* Household Treasury.

83 *Nineteenth-century irons: below, iron box iron with wood handle, in the North of England Open Air Museum, Beamish Hall: bottom, cast-iron flat iron of 1900, widely used for many years before and after that.*

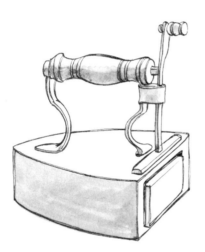

remain in use, being easier to heat on a gas ring as late as last century and even, in some cases, surviving well into the present century for use if, for example, the electric iron failed. There were many special irons also in use, the most famous being the goffering iron, made in many forms and particularly popular for dealing with the elaborate frills and pleating of women's nineteenth-century underwear.

The gas iron appeared about the middle of the nineteenth century, and continued to be used until the 1930s, as did various irons fuelled with oil, paraffin, petrol and other means. The electric iron existed in the USA from the end of the last century, but was slow to be adopted in Britain because of the slowness of electricity to come into the home. The modern type of steam iron, like other innovations in the washing and care of clothes, was a latecomer, not becoming widely popular until the 1950s.

Dyeing and Colour Problems

Dyeing has been practised since prehistory and, like the crafts of spinning and weaving, continued with few fundamental changes over many centuries. The aims were always the same – to colour the whole fabric and not just decorate its surface, as a painter might or as early man had done when adorning his own body, but also to make the colour impervious to rain, sun and washing. These qualities were not attained with any confidence until the eighteenth and nineteenth centuries.

The original and for long the main dyes used were obtained from natural sources, such as berries, flowers, fruit, leaves, lichens, seaweed and wood. The chosen substance was at first mixed with a liquid to form a paste which was pressed into the material. By a process of trial and error, various methods were found to secure some degree of performance, non-fading and washability. Iron, earths, lime, gypsum, clay, coal and soot were found to be fast to light. Blood, saliva, wax and glue worked as binding agents. Later civilizations found that water-soluble substances were best, among them lichens, but permanence was elusive until science

84 *Seventeenth-century dyeing shown in a contemporary engraving.*

began to develop in the seventeenth century and led in that and the following century to the discovery that an additional substance was needed as a fixative. These varied according to the source of the dye and were called mordants, from the present participle of the French verb *mordre*, 'to bite'.

Early civilizations achieved considerable skill in dyeing by various means. The earliest extant dyed textiles were found in the tombs of ancient Egypt. Purple, obtained from mollusc shells, was among the colours most prized by the ancient Greeks and Romans, the latter designating it the royal colour and setting a tradition which lasts to the present time. Medieval paintings and illuminated manuscripts provide dazzling evidence of the wealth and variety of colour achieved in the Western European countries; Florence, as well as being a great centre for painters, was also the leading centre for dyeing and the main source of developments which were as important to the history of dress as were the textiles themselves.

Many endeavours were made to evolve synthetic dyes which would add to the choice of colours available, but success here was not achieved until 1856, when Sir William Henry Perkin (1838–1907) produced the first aniline dye. The chemical base so named had been distilled from indigo with caustic potash in 1841 by another chemist, the term 'aniline' being derived from the Sanskrit name for the indigo plant. Since then, however, aniline has mainly been made from coal-tar. Perkin called his first dye mauvine and after him various scientists produced a number of other dyes, the best known being magenta.

These were brilliantly coloured, but the problem of making them fast to washing, cleaning, sunlight and wear-and-tear took further time to solve and success was not fully achieved until the middle of the present century, by which time new synthetic fabrics had brought in further colour problems.

8
Gradual Revolution in the Nineteenth Century

The Sewing Machine

Though spinning and weaving were mechanized in the eighteenth century and cotton mills were turning out vast quantities of fabrics before 1800, the greatest of all obstacles to the speedier, simpler production of clothes remained. Interminable hand sewing was the only way of putting garments together, and this continued for another half-century before a solution to the problem was found in an efficient, acceptable sewing machine. It was a mighty instrument of change in clothing. 'The sewing machine', say the authors of *The Needle is Threaded*, 'would have led to a revolution in tailoring as inevitably as the electric telegraph revolutionized communications and the steam engine travel.'

The revolution was needed most of all in the newly growing industrial areas, among the work-people there, who had neither time nor money for the traditional bespoke tailor or dressmaker, nor the facilities for home manufacture of clothing which had supplied many needs in the more domestic settings of the past. Now women and children as well as men were being drawn into the ever-demanding mills. It was to the working classes of all grades that the first machine-made clothing was directed. The rich and fashionable were too deeply attached to the bespoke tailor or private dressmaker to be tempted to the ready-made trade for many years to come.

It would be highly satisfactory to be able to record that it was to rescue women from their thraldom to the perpetual routine of hand-sewing that the sewing machine was invented, but unfortunately it did not happen that way.

As with other great advances in clothes manufacture in the following century, war was the main inspirer. Uniforms were needed for armies and making them was a heavy tax on time and energy. Another need was that of American whale fishermen, who needed particularly tough, warm garments to protect them while pursuing their trade.

It was, however, an Englishman who first produced a machine to do stitching, though final success eluded him. Thomas Saint was in 1790 granted a patent for a machine for sewing leather and his drawings show a number of features essential to the modern sewing machine. He seems, however, not to have put his idea to practical use.

The first man to obtain a patent and put it to use was a poor French tailor, Barthélémy Thimmonier, who by 1831 had 80 of his machines making uniforms for the French army. These machines were destroyed by angry mobs who thought their jobs in tailoring were being threatened. Thimmonier, however, persisted and took out patents in England in 1843 and in the USA in 1850, for machines which could deal with anything from muslin to leather, but he was overtaken by other inventors.

The first practical sewing machine to capture the market and hold a main part of it from then till today was Isaac Merrit Singer's, patented in America in 1851, when the firm that bore his name was founded. His machine was seen in America in 1855 by Robert Symington, a member of the Market Harborough corset-manufacturing company, who in the next year brought three Singers to the cottage workrooms of the family business, presided over by his

Shafting, Belting, Shaft Hangers, Belt Shifters, Drivers,
Pulleys, Floor Stands, Stools, Foot Motors, Electric Motors,
etc.   Factory Tables of every description.

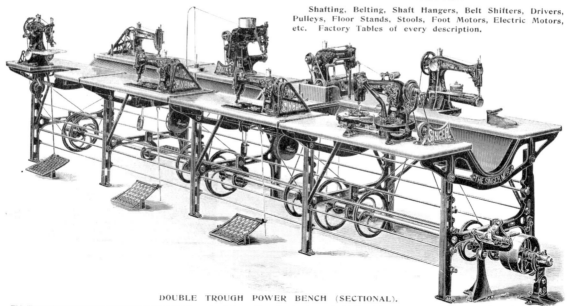

DOUBLE TROUGH POWER BENCH (SECTIONAL).

This illustration shows our Double Trough Power Bench, constructed upon the sectional system.   In this Bench there are two machines to each section and, as in the Single Bench, it can be extended to any length : the trough is the same width as in the single Bench, viz., 16¼ in., and the table tops are each 16¼ in. wide, making a Bench 48⅞ in. in width, while the sections may be had in three lengths, viz., 36 in., 42 in., and 47 in.   This Double Bench is adjustable in height from 28¼ in. to 32¼ in. from the top of the tables to the floor.

In this Bench as in all others, the utmost care has been exercised in preserving strength and rigidity, with the result that while design and appearance have not been sacrificed, any of our Sectional Benches are fully capable of carrying any of the large sewing machines which we manufacture, without loss of stability or the sacrifice of any good qualities.

Estimates for Factory Re-organisation Work Free.

85 *Above: industrial sewing soon after the end of the nineteenth century: Singer's Double Trough Power Bench, designed to carry two machines to each section, and to be extended to any length.*

86 *Below: these early sewing machines were steam-driven, operated by standing workers: a busy workroom of the 1850s.*

mother. There in 1856 the sewing machine was used for one of its most necessary purposes, stitching the innumerable bones into the formidable corsets worn by women of that time. Despite some protests from work-people on the usual grounds of their jobs' being threatened, he succeeded in getting them used. Women, the greatest users of the domestic sewing machine, can therefore claim that it was first used in their service.

To the benefit of women was also the fact that one of the first things Singer did on becoming established in Britain was to open retail shops, devoted entirely to selling his machines. The first opened in Glasgow in 1856 and others followed rapidly. By the 1870s there were over 160 Singer shops throughout Britain, and there are Singer shops today. It is likely that this was the start of multiple shop trading, which was to become an important feature of the ready-made clothing trade.

Other manufacturers quickly followed Singer into the sewing machine market, which became big business, with machines for factories, workshops and private homes.

87 *An early hand sewing-machine rouses interest.*

Mass-production for Men

A small amount of ready-made clothing had existed before the advent of the sewing machine, consisting, in the men's clothing area, mainly of roughly made underwear and shirts, crude outerwear generally called 'slop' clothes, and some heavy coats and cloaks, the last made by tailors when normal business was slack. But substantial developments in ready-to-wear could be made only with the sewing machine, and they were quick to begin. The first ready-made clothing factory was that of John Barran, which in 1856 at its factory in Leeds acquired between 20 and 30 Singer machines. Two years later they introduced another innovation – a band-knife which could cut through two dozen double thicknesses of heavy cloth at a time, thus immensely speeding up the cutting of clothes. It was based on a band-saw originally used for cutting furniture veneers, but was widely adopted by the clothing trade. At first sewing machines were operated manually, but in 1879, when the oscillating shuttle was introduced, they could be worked on power instead of treadle – first with a steam or gas engine, later by electricity or petrol.

Once sewing became mechanical, production increased rapidly. There were seven or eight

88 *Early nineteenth-century dress for men, women and boys. Panoramic views from the* Cyclopaedia of British Costume, *1833.*

clothing factories in Leeds in 1881, but by 1891 there were 54. With this expansion came another innovation – the establishment and growth of men's and boys' speciality shops, selling factory-made clothing. From these grew in turn multiple shop groups. By 1900 there were at least 22 of these, with over 50 branches each. The chief ones were Hepworths, G. A. Dunn and Bradleys of Chester.

At the same time Co-operative Societies joined the ever-growing ranks of manufacturing clothiers and the combination of their efforts with those of the multiples and small-scale retail men's outfitters meant that in the last quarter of the nineteenth century there was a great increase in the production and distribution of men's factory-made clothing to the working classes. These clothes were now more usually made of woollen materials, which were progressively replacing the cotton corduroy, leather and moleskin (which meant a kind of cotton fustian with a smooth surface) jackets, trousers and sometimes suits of the mid-

nineteenth century workman, now increasingly a city-dweller. This was possible because woollen fabrics had become less costly with the general change-over to machine spinning and weaving, in which wool had lagged behind cotton, mainly because of technical difficulties.

In addition a big stimulus had been given to the reduction of prices by the introduction of shoddy. 'Shoddy' was originally not a term used to describe any inferior fabric, as it is today; it meant a particular material made by the use of a rag-tearing machine called a 'devil'. This was a drum-shaped machine with teeth and was first introduced in 1801 but greatly improved later.

89 *A Lancashire working man and his family at home in 1861. He wears the new loosely cut, short jacket suit. From a painting of the time.*

Wool rags were fed into it and shredded as the drum revolved. The resultant pulp would then be spun, along with some new wool, into a less costly material suitable for the cheap suits in demand for working men. A rather better-quality blend was called 'mungo'. Shoddy commanded an extensive market by the later nineteenth century. It was, however, ousted by the introduction of many new types of fabric during the present century.

90 A Punch *view of the ordinary Victorian household, 1845. The husband wears the checked trousers which were becoming popular, and his* cap is unconventional. His wife's full skirt is moving towards the crinoline of ten years later.

Taken together, these events mean that since the arrival of the sewing machine there had been something approaching a revolution in the making and materials of much of the ordinary man's dress, especially among the growing number of small tradesmen, skilled factory workers and office workers. These had hitherto tended to seek out the cheaper bespoke tailors, an approach which was laborious and not always very successful. Census figures of the second half of the last century show a massive change-over in employment from the traditional tailor to the clothing factory tailoring worker. Thus in 1851 there were only 935 men and 29 women tailors employed in Leeds. By 1871 there were 1,523 men and 413 women, in 1881 2,148 men but 2,740 women and by the turn of the century less than 6,000 men and over 14,000 women.

When factory-made men's clothing was developed after the advent of the sewing machine, the most interesting point is exactly what was made. It is impossible to think of the factories of that time being able to produce the tailored frock coat or tail coat then worn by middle- and upper-class men, from the rich to the quite modest city worker. But as the populace was drawn increasingly into towns, to the factories

91 *More checked trousers and varying styles of coat in two items from an Edinburgh series* Modern Athenians, *of the 1840s.*

which as steam power developed had to be built near coal fields and therefore away from the traditional rural areas of population, the long-established short coat of the working man, sometimes known as a sack, underwent a change.

At the beginning of this vogue, in the 1850s, the short coat was loose and shapeless, made of tweed or serge, but it became finer, neater and better fitting and was worn with trousers, usually in a contrasting dark material, checked, plaid or striped. By the 1860s the outfit was widely accepted as informal wear by a considerable range of ordinary men. By the 1870s a waistcoat was added and it became, and was called, a suit. This type of suit, though a generally accepted mode of dress, was for a time

92 *The short-jacket suit is worn by the bus conductor in this 1860* Punch *cartoon on the recurrent theme of the absurdity and inconvenience of the crinoline in everyday life.*

regarded by gentlemen as appropriate only for morning, country or sport. But by the last years of the century, as the lounge suit, it was making solid inroads into the domination of the frock coat for business and general wear.

The top hat, which was the accompaniment of the dress of the Victorian man of any substance, was, surprisingly to many of us, worn by all classes. The first policemen wore top hats and swallow-tail coats, records Agnes Allen in *The Story of Clothes*, and she also notes that in summer white trousers completed this outfit. Top hats were also worn by many other groups of working men and were kept on at work.

The most usual top hat was black, fitting in with the dark colours worn by Victorian men on most occasions. Sometimes, however, the top hat was grey or white, the grey version surviv-

93 *Top hats for all – a family group of the 1860s.*

ing today as correct wear for formal occasions, along with the morning suit, now also a special-event garment. The frock coat disappeared early in the present century.

With the short jacket suit, which was informal in style, top hats were clearly unsuitable and from the 1850s there existed the round, low-crowned bowler, so named from William Bowler, who first manufactured it. It was made in grey, brown and black, with various small differences in the shape of the brim, from curly to straight, but the black version finally prevailed. Contrary to the top hat, which descended from the gentleman to policemen and workmen, the bowler rose in status. From being casual wear it came to be, like the short jacket suit, generally worn on everyday occasions by nearly all men by the turn of the century. It was

also known as a billycock and, in America, as a derby. The soft felt hat, even less formal, appeared in the 1880s and, for summer, the hard straw hat or 'boater' and the soft Panama. Caps, which probably derived from traditional unfashionable but practical wear of country-men, became popular as sports clothes became a feature of men's dress towards the end of the nineteenth century. Tweed and wool hats also came in, the former's most famous early wearer being Sherlock Holmes.

In recent years the hat has disappeared from many masculine wardrobes, so far as everyday dress is concerned.

94 *Winter fashions of 1834 show top hats universal among men.*

95 *A top hat was even worn for gardening, as seen in J. C. Loudon's Gardener's Magazine, 1832, which recommends mowing in an advertisement as 'an ideal recreation for a Gentleman'.*

96 *More top hats as a feature of men's dress in 1858; here are also shown the popular frock coat, an overcoat and the long jacket which was to become the short lounge-suit jacket.*

Slow Reform for Women

By the twenties of the nineteenth century women's dress was changing from the spare, classic up-and-down simplicity which had prevailed since the last years of the previous century. It was gradually becoming fuller-skirted, with puff sleeves reappearing and increasing in size, corsets becoming once again formidable figure-controllers, waists nearing their natural place. This soon led to the notorious tight-lacing which became widespread and was not limited to the wholly leisured and fashionable, but spread to women of all classes; a small waist was a special vanity.

Colours became stronger at the same time, with magenta, purple, bright green and blue among the favourites, supplanting the previous pastels. Fabrics of heavy types were also to the fore, among them plush, velvet, heavy woollen and silk and brocade. Trimmings and embroideries, beading, fringes and all kinds of elaboration were in favour again. Buckram stiffened skirts and sleeves and petticoats became heavier, wider and more numerous. The ostentation of the Victorian woman was on its way and was an effect much sought after by the middle classes. The poor could not compete – as they had been able to do to some degree in the time of simple cottons.

This trend continued, and when the sewing machine became a reality in the 1850s its arrival was declared by many to be providential: never had there been so many yards of petticoats and skirts to be hemmed by the tired fingers of dressmakers and their apprentices. The population was rising, prosperity was increasing, so the toil of hand-sewing became heavier.

The use of the sewing machine for making clothes for women was, however, very different and more complicated than for men. For one thing, women's clothing manufacture did not go into factories as did men's. Partly this was

97 *Nineteenth-century fashion changes: a dress, tippet and bonnet of 1815–20 are, apart from the high bonnet, simple and figure-clinging.*

98 *By 1830 a transformation had taken place:
an extreme example of fashion, not for the
ordinary woman.*

99 *By 1836, however, fullness was all, with the weekly* Belle Assemblée *showing this at a time when keeping up with fashion was influencing many more women.*

because the kind of uniformity expressed in the early men's clothing from factories had no attraction for women. But in addition the only equipment needed for a worker on women's dressmaking was the treadle or hand sewing machine, and employers found that it was easier and more profitable for dressmaking to be done by outworkers, who bought, hired or were supplied with such machines and worked at home. This meant that many women who could not go out to do a day's work in the factory – the old, infirm or those with young children – could pursue their work at home. Singer's chain of shops selling his machines and similar arrangements made by other sewing machine manufacturers made it easy for the family woman also to buy a machine and pursue her traditional sewing for her household by speedier and more effective methods. The visiting dressmaker, the source of many families' stocks of clothing, was also able to operate more effectively in this way and continued to be an important source of the middle-class woman's wardrobe.

To help such women, especially the ordinary ones who were not affluent, the paper-pattern business boomed. In August 1850, *The World of Fashion*, a monthly periodical, began to include

100 *Full skirts were general by the early 1850s. This picture* Low Life *shows a seamstress dressing for the evening and is companion to an* exotic one called High Life, *both dated before the sewing-machine was introduced.*

a collection of paper patterns. It promised a great variety of patterns for garments for every possible occasion and this was a big circulation booster. Other magazines followed and in 1860 *The Englishwoman's Domestic Magazine*, Samuel and Isabella Beeton's very popular production, arranged a pattern service. In 1873 Butterick's famous American pattern service set up in business in England in a big way, with Regent Street premises where they employed between 30 and 40 assistants by the 1880s and with a factory at Chalk Farm. Paper patterns became available everywhere and though the various kinds and degrees of dressmaker remained the chief makers of women's clothes at all social levels, a revolution in dress was none the less on its way.

The first steps in ready-made clothing for women had, in fact, been made by the mid-1850s, even before the sewing machine came on the scene. Many of the larger draper's shops had acquired their own workrooms and dress-making staff, coinciding with the great growth of shopping among middle-class women in Victorian England. At quiet times of the year they would make stock capes, mantles and other garments which did not need individual fitting. There also came into existence a curious item

described variously as part-made and un-made and consisting mainly of dresses of which sometimes the skirt was completely made up, the bodice only partly stitched, but so designed that it could be adjusted to fit various sizes and shapes of women. Sometimes the material and trimmings only were supplied for the bodice, but Jay's mourning service offered a 'self-expanding bodice' to suit all 'at a moment's notice'.

A few manufacturers also came into existence for ladies' wear when the sewing machine arrived. The most notable of them was Sélincourt and Colman, who opened in the City of London in 1857, making costumes and children's clothes as well as coats, waterproofs and shawls and selling to leading stores from the start. As Sélincourt, they still exist today with the same high reputation and many of the same customers.

101 *A wholesale pioneer in good-quality ready-to-wear ladies' dress was Selincourt, originally Sélincourt & Colman. Here in a centenary brochure issued in 1957, they reproduced some of the waterproof cloaks of their first year. Included in the booklet are illustrated Rules of Measurement of chest, neck, sleeve and length.*

ỌSBORNE.

(PLAIN IN TWEED ONLY)

BLUE TICKET QUALITY

| Nº 31 | length 52 inches | fullness 172 | 18/- |
| 32 | 56 | 188 | 19/6 |

ORANGE TICKET QUALITY

| Nº 131 | length 52 inches | fullness 172 | 21/6 |
| 132 | 56 | 188 | 23/6 |

ẸDINBORỌ'

(BRAIDED SHOULDER, LENGTH 54 INS)

| Nº 81 | BLUE TICKET QUALITY | 19/6 |
| 181 | ORANGE TICKET QUALITY | 22/9 |

Multiples did not enter the women's market nearly as early as they did that of men. In the North, co-operatives did a certain amount of business among the women in industrial communities from the last years of the nineteenth century, but the first important group was Fleming Reid, which opened its first branch in 1881 and by 1895 had over 75 branches, only Hepworths being larger in the men's area. By 1910 Fleming Reid had over 200 branches, with a strong bias towards hosiery, knitwear and underwear, but catering widely for the general needs of ordinary women.

Most of ordinary women's clothing was, however, provided by the stores. Mainly these were originally drapers, but they expanded from the middle of the nineteenth century, were up-market in their trends and met the needs of a growing army of middle-class women who were strongly imbued with the Victorian obsession with appearances – with embodying the prosperity of the family, the significance of its place in the world, supported by the *paterfamilias* in his rising business or trade, and intent that their clothes, houses, furnishings should live up to current ideals.

With railway travel easing, buses plying busily in London (there were 3,000 horse omnibuses in London in 1853, each carrying 300 people a day writes Alison Adburgham) the attractions of a day's shopping in London were made available and women seized the opportunity. Shops expanded, grew into stores with 20 or 30 departments and became more attractive, with rest rooms, tea rooms, solicitous attention from staff all adding to the customer's enjoyment.

But clothes still tended to be made mainly by the dressmaker with her own premises, by the visiting dressmaker or in the large made-to-order departments of stores, so far as the middle as well as the upper classes were concerned. The idea of standardized clothes, of mass-production, was distasteful; ready-made was regarded as 'cheap and nasty'.

From the mid-1830s photography had been providing for the first time pictures showing clothes as they really looked on the people who chose and wore them. On the whole Victorian women present an awesome sight when recorded in this way instead of in the flattering fashion-plate. From before the crinoline era – the mid-1850s to the mid-1860s – to the end of the century the panoply of skirts and drapery, layer upon layer, firmly held out by crinoline, bustle, petticoats and other stiffening, is made more overwhelming by the amount of trimmings and decoration strewn and draped over it. There seems no end to the fringes and edgings, beads and bugles, ruchings and bows, loops and swirls to which skirts are subjected. The sewing machine had a lot to answer for. It was not till the next century that simplicity returned to women's dress.

Several attempts to rationalize women's dress were made in the course of the nineteenth century. When, in 1851, Mrs Amelia Bloomer, an American journalist, endeavoured to launch in Britain the outfit which acquired her name but was in fact designed by her friend Elizabeth Smith Miller, it was a complete failure, achieving its only immortality through cartoons in *Punch*. Fifty years later, however, it was adapted as a cycling costume and was worn quite widely by ordinary women as well as by extreme reformers. Gustav Jaeger did better in the 1880s with his gospel of sanitary woollen clothing, but his first disciples were not among ordinary people but among the highly fashionable, from Oscar Wilde to Bernard Shaw. William Morris endeavoured to lead clothing back to 'nature' and the simplicity thought to be characteristic of ordinary people in bygone times, but his loose, hand-made tweeds roused the scorn of the working man of the 1880s and 1890s, intent on being well-turned out by the main multiple tailors in the dignity of the orthodox suit, off-the-peg from one of the new big men's outfitting groups. His theories of aesthetic dress for women were followed by the upper-crust fashionable, but not by the ordinary woman. The nineteenth century in fact ended with women's dress largely unreformed both in looks and in manufacture.

102 *Mrs Amelia Bloomer could not rationalize Englishwomen's dress, but she added a word to the language. Here a reproduction of an authentic sketch of 'the new costume', as shown in an American periodical and reproduced in England's* The Home Circle.

Sweated Labour

In the mid-nineteenth century it might easily have been anticipated that the future of clothes would be a smooth progress towards supplying everyone's needs at lower prices. The mills and factories were pouring out an ever-increasing flow of inexpensive cottons of every type, the most practical material for the ordinary woman's everyday dress and for men's shirts. Wool had moved to factories for weaving and the newer 'shoddy' was providing a useful substitute for the traditional costly fabrics, so that the working man and his family could dress better at less cost. The sewing machine was sewing a finer seam than almost any hand-sewer could and was also doing so infinitely more quickly, thus easing the lot of tailor, dressmaker and the woman-at-home. Clothing factories were making major inroads into the lower-priced men's market and were increasing supplies and reducing costs of all underwear and accessories, which had been so burdensome when done by hand.

In spite of this the picture was not on the whole a happy one, except perhaps for the owners of the factories and mills. They soon found that semi-skilled or unskilled labour could carry out much of the work hitherto handled by skilled clothing workers and that such labour could cost much less. The general principle in industry was still to hire as cheaply as possible and get as many hours' work out of

103 *Cruikshank's view of the sweating system as it affected the poor family, as early as May 1828.*

employees as possible – which in the nineteenth century was not unusually the round of the clock, and even overtime on top of that.

At this time of low wages and exploitation of the labouring classes the clothing trade rapidly became notorious. Another major problem was the pouring into Britain (and also America) of Jewish immigrants fleeing from the Russian pogroms which from 1881 drove them from their homes and which spread to other areas of Eastern Europe. The Jews had traditionally been the tailors of Europe, probably because this trade called for the minimum of equipment and could be carried out anywhere, even though the people concerned might be harried over the earth; clothes were always needed, wherever they were.

104 *Factory children being driven out to work in the cotton factories in 1840. From an engraving.*

The immigrants, arriving in most cases derelict and jobless, were of necessity open to exploitation in the growing clothing trade, which they entered in every kind of capacity, as factory workers, outworkers, one-man businesses, family production units. Being skilled and clever, they frequently made good, and many of the 'giants' of the vast twentieth-century fashion trade trace their origins back to those struggling immigrants of last century.

For the moment, however, the chief effect of the invasions was further to dislocate the clothing trade. 'Side by side with the factories there was growing up that army of underpaid, over-

worked men, women and children, whose
existence came with such a shock to the pioneer
reformers of the 'eighties, when the "sweating
problem" was first heard of', writes S. P. Dobbs
in *The Clothing Workers of Great Britain*.
Sweated workers were employed in a great
number of industries and trades, old and new;
one of the biggest was the manufacture of
clothing.

Although factory production of clothes was,
apart from underwear, accessories and heavy
garments, mainly concerned, round the mid-
nineteenth century at any rate, with industrial
areas and the working class market, and mainly
men, the problems of sweated labour and of
immigrant workers affected all classes of trade.
Even top-class men's tailors would send out
simpler parts of work to the innumerable scattered workshops, outworkers and small
contractors who have been part of the clothes
manufacturing trade ever since then, and still
are. It has remained a notoriously badly organized trade, and underpaid workers are still a
problem today. After the Jews came other
immigrants, Pakistanis and Cypriots being prominent among them in recent times.

105 *The sweating system: the cheap tailor and
his workers in a grim commentary by Leech in
1845.*

Protest against sweated labour in the clothing industry grew. Its momentum, however,
was impeded by the lack of organization which
has always beset the industry. The most notable
move was the *Daily News* Anti-Sweating Exhi-
bition of 1906, organized by J. J. Mallon and A.
G. Gardiner, the paper's editor. Opened by
Princess Henry of Battenburg, it drew attend-
ances of 30,000 people during its six-weeks'
duration at the Queen's Hall, the famous London hall just north of Oxford Circus which was
destroyed by German raids in the Blitz of the
Second World War. It led to the formation of
the National Anti-Sweating League, aimed at
establishing minimum wages, and to the setting
up of a House of Commons Select Committee to
investigate the whole subject of home work in
the clothing trade.

When close investigation of sweated labour
was carried out in, for instance, the book
Makers of our Clothes by Mrs Carl Meyer and
Miss Clementine Black, in 1908, it revealed a

stream of cases of outworkers making women's elaborate lace-trimmed and tucked blouses and underwear of that and previous times for payment which worked out in pence for a garment, and a few shillings for a full round-the-clock working week.

The problems presented by the production of women's clothing since the introduction of the sewing machine are so complex that one would need an entire volume to deal adequately with the subject.

Changes and upheavals have continued to beset the clothing industry ever since then. In the 1980s it is alarming to know that the Low Pay Unit should campaign to put an end to sweated labour, with special attention to the dress industry, where there are still women working at home for such pay as 20p an hour. In a major 1979 survey on working at home it was found that 'slave labour' wages were on the increase. Of cases it examined, usually of women unable to work out of the home and needing to supplement the family income, more than half were earning less than 40p an hour and

106 *Overworked women toiling in a dressmaker's workroom in the West End of London: from a working-man's magazine of 1858.*

two-thirds less than 6op an hour. The goods they made were not cheap, and many different sections of the clothing trade, including some at the top of the market, were guilty of employing them – and still are.

The New Uniformity

The dress of Victorian men of all classes represents a process of adjustment to a time of widespread and vast economic, industrial, commercial, scientific and social developments. It progresses logically, with the lounge suit and bowler hat replacing the frock coat and top hat from the 1880s, sports jackets likewise indicating a more relaxed mood. But the dress of women during the second half of the last century seems on a general survey to bear no relation to any of these factors or to the great changes that were then taking place in the position of women.

107 *Typical dress for men in the late nineteenth century, when ready-made clothes had developed greatly: from the catalogue of a Ludgate Hill shop.*

While what men wore maintained a considerable uniformity, practicality and an increasing degree of functional simplicity, Victorian women indulged in a series of the most fantastic extravagances of attire seen since medieval times. Then, only the wealthy few had been affected, but now women of all classes succumbed to some of the most extraordinary distortions of their natural shape that had ever been seen. Queen Victoria and Florence Nightingale indeed rejected the crinoline, but factory girls and other working women of many types wore it, even in a china factory where the contraption swept breakable goods off shelves quite regularly. Bustles were so popular in the

108 *Fashionable dress for women in 1857 reached the heights of absurdity.*

1870s and 1880s that all kinds of devices were contrived to throw out the figure to the rear. They were mass-produced, cheap, and worn everywhere.

All this was in the second half of the century, when the women's movement was progressing vigorously in its aims of securing for women a more responsible place in society, some degree of legal authority in the family, better education, more job opportunities, and admission to professions. It was the time when the Marriage and Divorce Bill was passed in 1857, with amendments in 1858, 1884 and 1896; the time of the Married Women's Property Acts of 1870,

109 *A study in contrasting dress in the 1850s. A lady in a wide-sweeping crinoline visits a labourer's cottage and meets the family in their simple attire.*

1881 and 1882. It was the time when women battled their way into the universities, first became doctors. They went to work in greater numbers; there were 17,566 women shop assistants in 1861 and 20,166 by 1871. Women clerks first appeared in the census in 1861, when there were 5,989 of them. This had risen to 17,859 by 1891.

130

110 *Under the crinoline skirt: a print of the 1860s.*

111 *Crinolines were worn as a matter of course by the majority of middle-class women. This is a photograph of a family group of 1865.*

But there was no accepted business or professional woman's dress, no working uniform or style suited to practical needs. On the contrary these women who went out into the main new spheres, mostly male monopolies in the past, followed current fashion more sedulously than ordinary women had previously done. They used the increased clothes production made possible by the sewing machine and other moves into mechanization to help them to conform to singularly impractical styles of dress. These were styles still set by the leisured woman, mostly purposely ostentatious.

Ray Strachey, in *The Cause*, her history of the women's movement in Britain as seen in the 1920s, argues that the reason for this was that the Industrial Revolution had led to a decline in the economic importance of women, reducing them from craftswomen to unskilled labour, in the home robbing the married woman of her traditional part as colleague and partner of her husband, and leaving her no more to do than present to the world the success and prosperity of her husband. She had to show that she did not need to work. Hence the plethora of elaborate, impractical Victorian fashions. The first women to strive for careers, for a share in public life and affairs, were dressed in the styles of the day. Dame Millicent Fawcett, then Millicent Garrett, is seen in early photographs in a crinoline. Emily Davies, founder of Girton, is smothered in the voluminous skirts and tight bodices of the early 1870s.

That, however, is not the whole or even the main part of the ordinary women's dress story of the late nineteenth century. These pioneer

112 *Crinolines were no obstacle to shopping: a scene in a busy London shop in the mid-nineteenth century.*

women were mainly of the upper or upper-middle classes – such dress was the way to corridors of power – so it could be argued that it was helpful to them to keep to accepted fashion standards. There were critics of late Victorian dress. Women were not all content with it. Gwen Raverat, in *Period Piece*, writes of a middle-class childhood in Cambridge in the later nineteenth century (she was born in 1883) and gives many complaints about the clothes then worn by women. Most 'brought discomfort, restraint and pain' and 'except for the most small-waisted, naturally dumb-bell-shaped females, the ladies never seemed … quite as if they were wearing their own clothes. For their dresses were always made too tight, and the bodices wrinkled laterally from the strain, and their stays showed a sharp edge across the middles of their backs.'

There was to be action as well as protests against the afflictions caused by Victorian clothing. Two important things happened in the 1880s which were due neither to fashion leaders nor to the crusading women, but which were between them to transform women's dress and have a large influence on women's lives in all classes. They were the invention of the tailored costume and of the 'safety bicycle' and they turned out to not be unconnected. Both originated in the late 1880s. The costume, which consisted of a skirt and a jacket, worn either with a plain shirt, similar to that of a man, or else a blouse which was often very frilly and decorative, has been said to have been originated by top dressmakers Redfern or Creed – it is uncertain which. Made of tweed, serge or some other woollen material similar to men's suitings, or linen for summer, it was adaptable to all styles and to all types of women. For it women went back to men's tailors, usually for the first time since the seventeenth century. The costume was worn for travel, sport, town or country, for leisure or for work.

113 *The bustle of the 1870s could look attractive on occasion. This is a country wedding dress of 1872–74 in beige.*

114 and 115 *A variety of contrivances helped Victorian women to create the extraordinary contortions of shape required by the fashions of* *the period. Here are two devices to create the bustles of the 1870s and 1880s.*

116 *More reasonable dress of the 1890s: a day dress of about 1895 could be worn today without arousing comment.*

The bicycle has been eulogized times without number as the great liberator of women, giving them undreamt of opportunities for getting out and about, enjoying a new independence. Its use began among middle-class and upper-middle-class women in the later 1880s, but it soon spread to nearly all classes – you could hire one for sixpence an hour. What did you wear? You could not have ridden it if the bustle had remained in fashion or if the crinoline had been revived, but for it the new costume was uniquely opportune. Skirts were still long, but they could be caught up to avoid wheels while retaining decorum. Some women wore the Bloomer outfit which had been scorned more than 30 years ago.

Women were also at this time playing games, to some extent under the influence of the various health campaigns which had been promoted. The skirt and shirt blouse provided the first advance towards practical sports dress. They appeared on tennis courts. When the first Girton girls played hockey in the 1890s they too wore this outfit, with the stiff collar and tie on the shirt blouse. Women started to play golf in the late 1880s and the first English golf championship for women was held in 1893. For it too the same outfit was worn.

It was probably before 1900 that the best known of all fashion figures and one cast in a new mould made her appearance in the USA and in Britain. She was the Gibson Girl, trim in blouse and skirt, the creation of American artist, Charles Dana Gibson. She became world-famous and remained so for years. The original was his wife, Irene, one of the Langhorne sisters, of whom another was to become Lady Astor MP. Today a sign on a road in Danville, Virginia, records the site of the house where Irene was born and the fact that she was the inspirer of the artist's 'celebrated style-setting Gibson Girl illustrations ... following their marriage in 1895'. On the stage the Gibson Girl won new fame by being impersonated by Camille Clifford, in New York in 1902 and London in 1904. The description is significant – it was probably the first time that the dress

ideal had been a 'girl' – and that in face of the Edwardian adulation of the mature woman. The 'young fashion' of the future was born.

By the end of the nineteenth century skirts still trailed on the ground at times, corsets were still too tight, but there were no more freak fashions and the Edwardian fashionable woman was not the model for other women to seek to follow. The New Woman had arrived and she was the ordinary woman, trim in her blouse and skirt or tailored costume, later called a suit.

About 1908, the next significant fashion change came and its acknowledged leader, Pierre Poiret, declared later that he had achieved 'the fall of the corset and the adoption of the brassière which, since then, has won the day. Yes, I freed the bust, but I shackled the legs' – a reference to the hobble skirt of his straight up-and-down fashion figure. But that problem was easily solved with a slit or two or a

117 *Young ladies of 1885 went to their drawing lessons in the rather formal dress which still persisted, but* Punch *did not find anything to ridicule in it, as in the past.*

pleat or two near the hem. The New Woman could deal with that.

What had happened was that ordinary dress was now everybody's dress. The 1914–1918 war is commonly regarded as a line of demarcation between old and new, past and present thinking on dress and its problems. It is not so. The change took place long before that so far as essentials were concerned. Future developments were to be towards ease, simplicity and comfort – things which fashion had disregarded for centuries, together with a disregard for the needs of the ordinary woman. Classless fashion was on its way ... and even unisex dress. But that is another story.

118 *In the same year, 1885, a Regent Street shop featured in the* Gazette of Fashion *what were described as 'some enterprising developments in* casual wear for men'. But the top hat is still included.

119 *The Gibson Girl – one of the drawings by
Charles Dana Gibson which made her famous,
and helped to revolutionize women's dress from
the end of the nineteenth century.*

Select Bibliography

ADAM, S. and S., *The Complete Servant* (Knight and Lacey, 1825).

ADBURGHAM, A., *Shops and Shopping, 1810–1914* (Allen & Unwin, 1946).

Shopping in Style (Thames & Hudson, 1979).

ASHLEY, M., *Life in Stuart England* (Batsford, 1964).

BAYNE-POWELL, R., *Housekeeping in the Eighteenth Century* (Murray, 1956).

BRYANT, A., *Protestant Island* (Collins, 1967).

Restoration England, revised edn (Collins, 1960).

BUCK, A., *Dress in Eighteenth Century England* (Batsford, 1979).

BYRDE, P., *The Male Image* (Batsford, 1979).

A Frivolous Distinction (Bath City Council, 1979).

CAMPBELL, R., *The Complete London Tradesman* (T. Gardner, 1747, reprinted by David & Charles, 1969).

Costume (Costume Society, 1980 and 1981).

CROW, D., *The Victorian Woman* (Allen & Unwin, 1971).

CUNNINGTON, C. W. and P., *Handbook of English Costume in the Seventeenth Century* (Faber 1955, reprint 1974).

CUNNINGTON, P., *Costume in Pictures* (Herbert Press, 1964, revised edn 1981)

CUNNINGTON, P., and Lucas, C., *Occupational Costume in England* (A.&C. Black, 1967).

DAVIS, D., *A History of Shops and Shopping* (Routledge & Kegan Paul, 1966, also Toronto University Press).

DEFOE, D., *A Tour through the Whole Island of Great Britain, 1724–6* (pub. 1725–7, reprinted Dent, 1962).

The Complete English Tradesman, 1727 (Reprints of Economic Classics, A. M. Kellie, 1969).

DOBBS, S. P., *The Clothing Workers of Great Britain* (Routledge, 1928).

FELL, S., *The Household Account Book of Sarah Fell*, ed. Norman Penney (Cambridge University Press, 1920).

FIENNES, C., *The Journeys of Celia Fiennes*, edited with an introduction by C. Morris, foreword by G. Trevelyan (Cresset Press, 1947).

FRASER, G. L., *Textiles by Britain* (Allen & Unwin, 1948).

GARLAND, M., *The Changing Form of Fashion* (Dent, 1970.)

GEORGE, Dorothy, *England in Transition* (1931, revised with additions Penguin Books, 1953).

GILCHRIST, A., *Mary Lamb* (W. H. Allen, 1889).

GRANT, Elizabeth, *Memoirs of a Highland Lady*, ed. A. Davidson (Murray, 1950).

HARRISON, M., *People and Shopping* (Benn, 1975).

HAYDEN, R., *Mrs Delany, her Life and her Flowers* (Colonnade, 1980).

HINDLEY, Charles (ed.), *Roxburghe Ballads* (Reeves & Turner, 1973–4).

HOLE, C., *The English Housewife in the Seventeenth Century* (Chatto & Windus, 1953).

JEFFERYS, J. H., *Retail Trading in Britain, 1850–1950* (Cambridge University Press, 1954).

KILPATRICK, S., *Fanny Burney* (David & Charles, 1980).

MAYHEW, H., *London Labour and the London Poor* (1851). As *Mayhew's London*, ed. P. Quennell (Pilot Press, 1949).

MITFORD, M. R., *Our Village, 1824–1832* (reprint Oxford University Press, 1945, 1982).

NORTH, Roger, *Lives of The Norths 1826*, new edn. ed. A. Jessop (G. Betton, 1890).

PLUMB, J. H., *Georgian Delights* (Weidenfeld, 1980).

ROSSBACH, van Rostrand, *The Art of Paisley* (Reinhold Co., New York, London, 1980).

SMITH, J. T., *Book for a Rainy Day* (Methuen, 1845, new edn. 1905).

Nollekens and his Times (Turnstile Press, 1828, reissue 1949).

STEWART, M., and HUNTER, L., *The Needle is Threaded* (Heinemann/Newman Neame, 1964).

STRACHEY, Ray, *The Cause* (G. Bell, 1928).

THOMPSON, F., *Lark Rise to Candleford*, as trilogy (Oxford University Press, 1982).

VERNEY, F. P. and M., *Memoirs of the Verney Family during the Seventeenth Century* (Longmans Green, 1928).

VON LA ROCHE, S., *Sophie in London, 1786.* Translated with introduction by Clare Williams, foreword by G. Trevelyan (Cape, 1933).

WATERSON, M., *The Servants' Hall* (Routledge and Kegan Paul, 1981).

WAUGH, N., *The Cut of Men's Clothes, 1620–1900* (Faber, 1964).
The Cut of Women's Clothes, 1600–1930 (Faber, 1968).

WEETON, Miss, *Journal of a Governess*, Vol. II, 1811–1825 (David & Charles reprints 1969; first pub. Oxford University Press, 1939).

WILKERSON, M., *Clothes* (Batsford, 1970).

WOODFORDE, J., *Diary of a Country Parson*, selected and edited by J. Beresford (Oxford University Press, 1933, paperback 1978).

WRAY, M., *The Women's Outerwear Industry* (Duckworth, 1957).

YARWOOD, D., *English Costume* (Batsford, revised edn 1977).
The Encyclopaedia of World Costume (Batsford, 1978).
The British Kitchen (Batsford, 1981).
Five Hundred Years of Technology in the Home (Batsford, 1983).

Index